The Road to
<u>Barkersville</u>
Watch Out for Kids

Ephriam B. Barker Clan
Chronicles

Ada F. Barker

CONTENTS

Prologue

Epilogue

Appendix

This book is for my children and grandchildren.
Dedicated to Mama and Papa:
Mary Henrietta Peterman and Ephriam Buck Barker,
and to my siblings whose stories are in this book.
Thank you all.

"Have confidence, but see in whom you place it"

A special thank-you to Alice, my brother Ted's wife, who put the entire family history on disks for me, and to their daughter, Patricia Barker Jones, for her incredible compilation of all the family's history; to my cousin Greta Barker Blair, whose research I depended on so much for its accuracy; and to Virginia Schneider, who did such a fantastic job researching the Barker and Peterman families. And to my brothers, Jackie, Ted, and Earl, who were so helpful in getting information and pictures to me. I appreciate all who helped in any way.

PROLOGUE

My ancestors arrived in America in the 1600s and settled in Virginia. The Washington county Surveyors Records places my lineage in Washington County in the 1700s.

Treasury warrants were given for tracks of land to men who fought in the American Revolution by the King of Great Britain's Proclamation of 1863 and the Virginia Land Warrant of May 1777.

Barkers from my lineage were awarded land by these warrants and consequently ended up owning several hundreds of acres in Washington County, Virginia.

These lands with appurtenances such as farm implements and animals, as well as slaves, were either sold or passed down in families, and that is how my grandparents, Rev. Campbell Heiskel Barker Sr. and Fairzina Jamima Good-Hensley, came in possession of a tobacco farm.

Campbell Heiskel Barker Sr.: born August 10, 1858, in Kinderhook Township, Washington County, Virginia; and **Fairzina Jamima "Gal" Good-Hensley**: born July 19, 1861, in Scott County, Virginia, were married in Abingdon, Virginia, on September 27, 1877—he was 19 years of age and she was 16. They had nine children:

Cordelia: born April 28, 1879

Henry Clay: born Dec. 12, 1881

Bertha Virginia: born Dec. 18, 1883

Campbell Heiskel Jr.: born Sep. 19, 1886

Benjamin Harrison: born Aug. 9, 1888

Ephraim Buck: born May 1, 1892

Seaton Graves Sr.: born Jan. 12, 1894

Lillie May: born May 10, 1896

Earl Clifton: born Aug. 9, 1899

At age forty, Rev. Campbell left the Methodist church and began preaching for the Baptists. He built his own **church** in 1890 and was pastor there until 1904. He performed many baptisms and marriages, including those of his own family.

It has been said that Rev. Campbell Barker was a gentle man of good nature, but he never backed away from standing up for what he thought was right. In his youth, he and his brother Jonathon traveled with a circus, singing and playing the banjo.

Fairzina's lineage is a long one in Virginia as well. Her father, **Lilburn Hensley**, was born in March of 1833 and died in 1904. Her mother, **Lucinda Good,** was born in 1835 and died in 1870.

Lilburn was not married to Lucinda, he was married to her sister **Mary,** but he had children by both women; Mary had nine and Lucinda had seven. Lucinda lived with Mary and Lilburn for a while and then lived next door to them. Mary and Lucinda died within two years of each other leaving small children behind. It is believed that nine-year-old Fairzina went to live with an older sibling.

Great-grandfather Lilburn also had children with **Nancy Carter** during the time he was with Mary and Lucinda, and he married her after they died. He fathered Nancy's son **Robert Carter**, the father of **A. P. Carter,** who began the original Carter Family with his wife, **Sara**. Robert also fathered **Ezra Carter,** who married **Maybelle Addington**, and they, along with their daughters, **Helen, June**, and **Anita**, became the "new" Carter Family.

Lilburn was certainly a very busy man, but he somehow found time to fight in the Civil War with Capt. William J. Smith's Co., Clinch Mountain Boomers, Virginia volunteers.

I begin the book with my paternal grandparents, Rev. Campbell H. Barker and Fairzina Jamima Hensley, leaving Virginia and coming to California. After that, it proceeds with stories from my parents, Ephriam B. Barker and Mary Henrietta Peterman, and their immediate family.

Father:
Ephriam Buck Barker: born May 1, 1892

Mother:
Mary Henrietta Peterman: born May 22, 1898

Children:

August Leonard: born Aug. 20, 1914

Elden Ephriam (Bud): born Oct. 31, 1916

Ruth Mary: born June 6, 1918

Earl Clifton: born Sept. 30, 1919

Edith Viola: born Dec. 10, 1920

John (Johnny) David: born April 10, 1922

Robert (Bobby) Granville: born Aug. 25, 1923

Theodore (Teddy): born Jan. 13, 1925

Patrick (Pat) Henry: born March 24, 1926

Campbell (Cam) Heiskel: born Nov. 5, 1927

Benjamin (Benny) Harrison: born Nov. 14, 1928

Darlene Virginia: born Aug. 31, 1930

Paul: born Dec. 17, 1931

Gloria: born Jan. 25, 1933

Jimmie & Jackie: born June 26, 1934

Franklin Delano (Skippy): born Dec. 9, 1935

Ada Florence: born April 28, 1938

Charles (Charlie) Louis: born Dec. 30, 1940

Susan (Susie) Jane: born April 12, 1942

At the end of the book, there will be additional information on births, deaths and marriages from this lineage.

A Sad Farewell

Fairzina stood on the stoop of the church, hesitant to leave the place that had been such a comfort to her. She didn't know what she would have done without its sanctuary after the death of her oldest daughter, Cordelia, who had died two years earlier from consumption at age twenty-five, and Cordelia's baby girl, Goldie, who also died that year.

She was finding it hard to say goodbye. She and her family were leaving the next morning, traveling all the way from Virginia to California. They might never return.

Fairzina's son Ephriam came quietly to her side. "Ma, we have to leave now. "

Fairzina nodded, and then held on to the strong arm her fifteen-year-old son held out to her. She was a little unsteady as they walked through the churchyard. She was a small woman, lately in poor health. That was why they were all leaving Virginia. With tuberculosis so prevalent there, Fairzina's doctor had urged her husband to take her to California where the climate was dry and warm and no damp would enter her lungs.

No one who knew Fairzina thought of her as frail because even when she was ailing she was feisty. But the fire that usually burned in her steel-blue eyes was dim today. Fairzina was subdued, hardly speaking a word to anyone. She had not taken the care she usually did in getting ready for church. Her dark hair, still wrapped in a bun from the day before, had come loose during the service. She had kept trying to put it in place, as if just discovering its condition.

Now, as she and Ephriam followed the other family members as they walked to their home, Fairzina hoped desperately that the move to

California would bring more joys than heartaches.

Campbell Heiskel Barker Family

That evening, a hush fell over the old farmhouse that usually rumbled with the many loud voices of its inhabitants. And even though Fairzina and Campbell's six children talked excitedly about going to California, Fairzina understood that it wouldn't be easy for them to leave the only home they had ever known. They must wonder, as she did, what awaited them so far away.

Another thing that added to the melancholy that hung over the departing family members — they were leaving loved ones behind. Henry Clay and his family would stay in Virginia, and Bertha and her family would be staying behind, as well.

Henry and his family stayed for supper that Sunday, and everyone tried to break the somber mood. Ephriam got out his father's banjo and tried to get a sing-along going, which was usual for family gatherings, but no one's heart was in it.

After Henry and his family left, Fairzina began to fill the tin washtub for the youngest children. She finished pouring in the last kettle of hot water, then turned to find eight-year-old Earl standing behind her, his eyes filled with tears, his chin quivering. Defiantly, he thrust out his jaw, narrowed his eyes, and said, "Ma, I don't see why we can't take everybody with us; they won't have no place to have Sunday supper anymore — I bet they'll even stop going to church if Pa ain't there. It just ain't right to leave them; they're our kin. Ain't right.

A Sad Farewell

I'm not gonna go."

"Now you listen here, Earl Clifton, you go wherever Pa and me take you." Fairzina gave him a swat on the behind, and he burst out bawling with greater wailing than the gentle swat warranted.

The noise brought the rest of family into the room.

"What's going on here, Fairzina?" Campbell asked, frowning at his wife.

"Ain't nothing. Just a boy who's getting too big for his britches." Fairzina gave Earl another swat. "Now you get your bath, and then get to bed."

"Ma, he's sad about leaving, and so am I," said eleven-year-old Lillie. The girl went to Earl and put her arm around his shoulder, trying hard to stifle the sobs that were choking her.

Their father spoke soothingly and led them out of the room.

"Look at me," he said, lifting their faces up. "You know that we all feel the same way you do. We all wish we could take everyone with us, but that's not possible. The only thing we can do is to keep praying that we'll all be back together some day."

He shooed them away, saying no more on the subject.

The whole family turned in early, but Fairzina wasn't tired. She sat in the aged oak rocker, where she had rocked all her babies, and stared into the empty fireplace. The light from the full moon flooded through the windows and beckoned her outside onto the porch. She picked up Bluebeard, the old black tomcat, and petted him, something she had never done before. He usually took off running when he saw her coming, having been swept off the porch too many times by her broom. This time, he lay in her arms, looking up at her as if he knew this was a final farewell. Fairzina gazed up at the stars, said a prayer for all she was leaving behind, and went back into the house.

Once in bed, she thought about the time she had moved into this house as a new bride. She was only sixteen years old then, but despite her youth, she worked hard to be a helpmate to Campbell. Even as a child, she had been solemn, which may have partly been caused by her family's situation. And she had been lonely as a child, even though she had nineteen siblings, of which seven were full brothers and sisters.

As she lay in her comfortable featherbed, her whole life flashed through her mind as if she were a drowning person—her unhappy childhood, her meeting Campbell, which she considered to be the best thing that had ever happened to her, the births of her children, and the deaths of those she loved.

She thought about the place they were going off to. She didn't know anything about California; she had never met anyone who had been there. The only thing she had heard about was the temperate climate, which her doctor said would be better for her lungs. But she was not thinking about her health now; she was thinking about the children she was leaving behind.

They had promised her that they would come for a visit as soon as it was possible, but she couldn't shake the feeling that she would never see them again.

Circa 1913.L./R. Carrie,Ada May,Henry Clay Barker, Ernest, Nina "Bettie", Ettie Elizabeth,Sylvester "Vester", Norman. Courtesy Glenna McClain.

California

Friends and family gathered at the train depot the next morning— an early morning in June 1907. Reverend Campbell's parishioners presented him with a basket of food to sustain the family on their journey. He had been their pastor for many years, and had been their savior, mentor, and friend. He had never hesitated, even on dark nights and foul weather, to come and pray with them through hardship.

The train was on time. Fairzina, Campbell and their children wrested themselves from their loved ones and climbed aboard. They settled into their seats as the train began chugging out of the station. No one spoke.

Ephriam gazed out the window at the mountains, fields and cows, and at the people in their new motorcars. He was excited, sad, scared. He had always loved adventure, and his father promised him that. They were bound for the great American West, still a raw new land. What greater adventure could a young man undertake than going to California? Ephriam had heard that there was still plenty of gold to be mined. He was willing to work hard; he had been working hard since he was a small child.

Yes, he was excited, but when he caught a glimpse of the mountains or a green field, he thought about the place he was leaving. The place where he was born, his father before him, his grandfather, and his four great grandfathers, and leaving the familiar made him nervous.

He loved their farm even though there was a lot of hard work to do, and his adventure seeking had gotten him into trouble many times. Like the time he was nine years old and was fishing with his brother Harrison in the creek that ran alongside their farm. The fish weren't biting very well, so he decided to go to the other side.

Ignoring his brother's calls of impending danger, he began to walk across a tree limb that had fallen across the creek bed, when the limb broke, sending him head first to the rocky bed below.

He was lucky that his brother Harrison was with him, or he would have bled to death. It was a terrible injury; his head was split wide open.

They were miles from a doctor, and when his father saw his condition, he didn't think Ephriam could make it through such a long ride being bounced around in a buggy, so he had to make a decision on what he could do to save his boy. He couldn't see any debris anywhere inside the skull and the rocks he fell on were cleansed by running water, so he did the only thing that he thought might save his boy—he gently pushed the skull back in place. Then his mother took one of his baby brother's diapers, soaked it in Z-M-O oil, and put it on the injury. It was a long convalescence, but he healed completely.

Of course, there were plenty of prayers, and his parents credited them for his miraculous recovery. But Ephriam Buck, the sixth child of Reverend Campbell and Fairzina Jamima Good Hensley, wasn't all that impressed with religion. He did try though—at the ages of five and six, he listened intently to every verse his father preached and memorized many, but the older he got, the more he questioned some of the stories. Then he was told he was not supposed to question the word of God. But it was his nature to question; he couldn't accept anything on faith alone. Sometimes this made him feel guilty, and he was sure a sinner's life was his destiny.

Ephriam looked across the aisle to where his folks sat with his youngest siblings, Lillian and Earl. His mother frowned; it had become her normal expression after losing her oldest child. She, too, was looking out the window and for a moment, the frown eased, replaced by a wistful stare.

His father sat beside his mother, playing a game with Earl and Lillie. He was smiling. His father did that a lot. He was a pleasant man, not an authoritarian by any means; he left the serious discipline of the children to their mother, who was good at dishing it out.

Fairzina often told her children: "It's your Pa's job to learn you about heaven, and it's my job to learn you how to behave so you'll get there."

Ephriam's two older brothers sat beside him—Cam, who was twenty-one, and Harrison, nineteen. They were sleeping.

Ephriam laid his head back, closed his eyes, and had almost drifted off to sleep when his younger brother Seaton, a very restless thirteen year old, tugged at his arm.

"Hey, Buck, when are we gonna get there?"

"We'll get there when we get there," Ephriam said.

"I met a U.S. Marshal up front. He's bringing the body of a bad guy that he had to kill back to Utah where he murdered up a gob of people. He has lots of real good stories."

"Well, don't be bothering him so much."

"I ain't bothering him; he likes me."

Ephriam shook his head. "Just sit down here and keep still for a while."

Seaton frowned and flopped down in the seat in front of Ephriam.

When they arrived at the depot in Salt Lake City, Utah, the family disembarked. Ephriam went to retrieve Seaton, who had wandered off to see the marshal again. When Ephriam got to them, a coffin was being brought down off the train. The handlers lost control, flipped the coffin over, and sent the body face up to the ground. The body was riddled with bullet holes—he hardly had a face. Seaton stayed calm and quiet for the rest of the trip.

The train took them to the small farming town of Clovis, California, with vast wheat fields that looked so beautiful to Ephriam as the train passed one after another. It looked like a good town to settle in. There would be plenty of work with all the farming, and there was a large mill that required a lot of workers.

During the gold rush, miners moved into the area to find their fortunes in the rivers and streams around the area. A few had claims that were profitable for a while, but there were no bonanzas. Of course, this place fit right in with Ephriam's dream of finding his own fortune in gold, and if he couldn't find it there, it wasn't far to the Sierras, in Nevada, where many had struck it rich in the gold and silver mines.

When the family got off the train, they went to the only hotel in town and took two rooms. This was the first time the family had ever stayed in a hotel, and Seaton and the younger children thought it a great adventure. All the family, especially Fairzina, enjoyed the meals that were served in the dining room. She smiled more in those few days than she had in years.

They were at the hotel for about a week when a local physician, whom they had met in church, offered them a small house on his farm in exchange for caring for his livestock. It was a lucky break, as they didn't have very much money left.

The boys had various jobs on the farm, and Reverend Campbell spent a lot of time at the Baptist Church, helping with anything he could. He made a tiny stipend teaching Sunday school and conducting any service that that the Pastor, who had recently gone through a bout of ill health, was unable to do. Campbell occasionally did carpenter work whenever he was lucky enough to get it.

Searching for Gold

They had only been in town a few weeks when Ephriam, who couldn't wait any longer to try for his fortune, cajoled his brothers Cam and Harrison into doing some gold panning along the river.

Ephriam was more excited than his brothers, who were skeptical that gold could still be found, but they were willing to give it try if for no other reason than to quell his incessant talk about gold. So the three put their equipment in gunnysacks along with some biscuit and bean sandwiches and a jug of water, and set out at daybreak.

They stopped and tried their luck at various spots, but after an hour or so at each with no sign of gold, they would move on. They did that until late afternoon, when Cam and Harrison began to complain that they were tired and hungry and were going home.

But Ephriam, who wasn't willing to give up just yet, did a little more inveigling. "Just one more try, and I promise that'll be it. We'll just go around the bend and then we'll call it quits, and I'll never ask you to come along with me again."

Cam and Harrison reluctantly gave in, and as they got around the bend, a stream of smoke arose from the cattails along the bank.

"Let's check this out and see who's here," Ephriam said.

They slowly went toward the smoke and as they got closer, the aroma of food cooking made them walk faster. They were hungry, as they had eaten their biscuits hours ago, and as their mother always said, "You boys have two hollow legs and a direct path to hell, 'cause that's where gluttony will get you."

As they drew closer, through the long fuzzy spikes of the cattails, they saw a man sitting on his haunches in front of a small campfire, stirring something in an iron skillet. When the little man with the long, straggly hair heard them, he grabbed a rifle from the ground beside him, and hopped up like a jack-in-the-box.

"Who's trespassin' on my property?" the toothless man called out, his words muddled.

He cocked the rifle, and Harrison and Cam took off running, but Ephriam stood his ground.

"Hey, we're not trespassing, we didn't know you were here; we've been doing some panning along the river, and we were just about ready to call it quits when we came upon you.

Is it all right if I come talk with you for a moment?"

"What fer? Ye ain't got no bidness with me. This'n here is my claim and yer not welcome here, so take yer tail out of here afore ye get a blast from ole Beulah." He stuck his jaw out, and his eyes—one brown, one blue—flashed in defiance.

"Okay, okay, but first hear me out. I only want to get your opinion on gold panning; I don't know anything about it, and you probably know everything there is to know. I'll bet you have some great prospecting stories to tell about this area."

The prospector lowered his rifle. Ephriam put his hands up, and walked up to the man.

"Yer damned straight I have some stories. I've been panning this-here river for nigh on to thirty years and watched all kinds of fellers, and one gal, come and go," he answered, then sat back down and put his rifle aside.

Ephriam cautiously sat down near the old man and extended a hand to him.

"My name is Barker—Ephriam Buck Barker."

The man shook his hand. "I'm Jasper J. Johnson, and this here is Beulah." He pointed to his rifle. "And my claim takes up this whole area as far as the eye can see and no varmint better ever try to jump my claim. This-here place is sacred to me; that's why I named 'er Jenny's Jewel, after my mama. She's the main reason I'm prospectin', and I'm not a gonna quit until I make enough to buy 'er the things she's deservin' of."

Ephriam liked the fighting spirit of the sun baked prospector, and the nobility of his reason for being there.

Jasper shared his greasy, burnt fried potatoes, rye whiskey and his plug of chewing tobacco with Ephriam, and they became friends from that day forward. Later, Ephriam heard from the people around town that this was unusual; they said that Jasper was definitely a loner and didn't like anyone even coming near his claim. Ephriam found that to be true the day he took Cam and Harrison to the claim and Jasper chased them off.

Ephriam spent his free time at Jenny's Jewel, learning about mining and listening to Jasper's stories. And although the little guy, who was as dried up as the many abandoned claims along the river, hadn't become rich yet, his enthusiasm never wavered. And with every story he told, Ephriam became even more excited about prospecting.

The family was in Clovis for less than a year when some people who had just come from Oregon told them of a little church there that needed a pastor. They convinced Reverend Campbell that it was a good community, and there would be a lot of work in the hop vineyards, the strawberry fields and the cherry orchards. The reverend informed his family that they would be leaving in June.

Soon after they had met, Jasper told Ephriam that he was expecting a letter from his mother, so whenever Ephriam went out to the claim, he would go by the post office to see if there was mail for Jasper. There had never been any mail, until that morning Ephriam was to inform Jasper that he would be leaving. Ephriam stuck the letter in his back pocket and hoped that the letter would be good news, making what he had to tell, easier for both of them.

Jasper greeted Ephriam with the usual enthusiasm and gave him a rusty tin cup filled with foul-tasting coffee.

"Buck, an idee came to me last night as I was ponderin' that maybe I should expand my claim. I thought maybe we could go check things out upstream a ways."

"Haven't you tried every place along this river already?"

"Yeah, but it won't hurt to go back again. Do ye think maybe we could do that? How about today? It's still early."

Ephriam stood up and threw the grounds from his cup into the fire. "I can't today, Jasper." He hesitated and then continued, "Jasper, I have something to tell you."

Jaspers excitement caused Ephriam even more despair and he forgot about the letter.

"What is it that ye gotta tell me?"

Ephriam sat back down and looking at the embers in the fire said, "Jasper, my family's going to be leaving for Oregon in a couple of days. There's supposed to be a church for my father there."

Jasper's jaw dropped, and he looked away. "Yer leavin' in two days?"

Ephriam nodded. Jasper turned and faced him with a look that Ephriam had only seen before on a doe he had wounded.

"Ye can't leave now; I'm tellin' ye Buck, I know we're gonna hit pay dirt here, real soon. Ye don't want to miss out on that, do ye?"

"I've no choice. I have to go with my family, Jasper. You understand that, don't you?"

While he was saying that, Ephriam remembered the letter.

"Jasper, I've got something for you." He gave the letter to Jasper, who laid it aside, not looking at it.

"Ye gotta stay, Buck. I know we'll be rich. Heckfar, I'll even make ye an equal partner. Now ye can't pass that up, can ye? Besides, what are ye gonna do in Oregon? Ain't nothin' there but rain; it rains all the time. Buck, if ye don't take me up on my offer, ye'll be kickin' yerself to kingdom come when ye find out 'bout my big bonanza."

Jasper kept begging him to think it over, and when Ephriam left that day, he could swear that he saw tears in those tired, squinty, little bloodshot eyes.

The next day Ephriam went to Jenny's Jewel, for what was supposed to be for the last time. He was sad as he left for claim that morning; he would miss old Jasper, his stories and his rye whiskey. Ephriam chuckled; the only thing he wasn't going to miss was Jasper's coffee that he boiled far too long, and was as thick and black as smoke from an old tire and tasted as such.

When Ephriam neared the camp, he expected to see Jasper sitting by his fire, but he wasn't there, and it didn't look like there had been a fire that morning.

He went to the shack that Jasper had thrown together with pieces of old tin and boards left at abandoned sites along the river. He pulled back the raggedy quilt that served as a door and found the willowy body lying on the dirty, old mattress that was on the ground.

Jasper was on his side, and when Ephriam turned him over, his eyes were open but there was no life in him. Sadness came over Ephriam, as he closed Jasper's eyelids.

"Jasper J. Johnson, you are no longer of this world, and as the Bible says: "From dust ye came, to dust ye shall return." Well, old friend, I imagine that the dust you return to will be gold dust."

The lifeless man had a piece of crumpled paper in one of his gnarled fists, and when Ephriam pried it loose from the grasping fingers, a small gold wedding ring fell from it, landing on a small picture that was laying near his side. An envelope lay near the picture, and it looked like the one that Ephriam had delivered to Jasper the day before.

Ephriam picked it up, smoothed out the paper and read it:

May 28, 1908

Dear Mr. Johnson:

I am sorry to inform you that your mother, Mrs. Jennifer Johnson, expired sometime during the night of May 25, 1908.

She suffered from senility and passed away in her sleep. I hope that it is of some comfort to you to know that she didn't suffer greatly.

We've taken care of your mother for the last year and although most of her memories had left her, she did keep your baby picture by her bedside and I feel that she did remember you.

I am enclosing the picture and her ring. That was all the dear lady had of any value.

Please accept our condolences, and we wish you well in your endeavors.

Sincerely,
Mrs. Ida King: Proprietor
Danby's Convalescent Home

Ephriam sat for a while just looking at the pitiful sight of the scrawny little man on the dirty mattress, and then he let out the tears — probably the only ones that would be shed for the lonely little prospector. And on that beautiful, sad day, Ephriam let go of all his dreams of finding gold.

Before leaving, he picked up the dog-eared baby picture and ring, to keep as mementos of the memory of his old prospecting buddy.

The Coroner's office said he died from natural causes, but the talk around town was that it was from a broken heart. They said that to lose his best friend and his mother at the same time was probably more than he could bear.

Jasper was buried three days later in potter's field, and Reverend Campbell led the service. All of the Barker family attended, and surprisingly, there were about twenty others at the service.

Ephriam went out to Jenny's Jewel the day after the funeral. He sat by the river, remembering the good times he had there with Jasper. In the babble of the running water, he swore he heard the old man's feeble voice begging him to stay. He was glad that they would be leaving the next morning, heading on to a new and hopefully better future.

Oregon

When the family arrived at Mt. Angel, the pastor job was already filled, but they stayed in that area for the next few years, following the hops, berries and fruit harvests. That's what they were doing in the summer of 1913, when they came to Hood River, Oregon.

Around the middle of August, the family arrived at the Simmons Ranch at Mission Bottoms and set up camp. Several other families had already set up camps and were waiting for the hops to start.

Ephriam's family set up their tents near the front of the camp, the only site left. People came early to get the best sites and left the ones at the front near the dusty road for the stragglers. Anyone camping there would inevitably have dust as part of their daily menu.

Excitement permeated the camp as people met others from all over the country. Hop picking was no fun, but some things in the camp were. The young people had the most fun meeting others their age, especially the opposite sex.

Their father went around the camp introducing himself to the other workers, like he always did whenever they arrived at a new camp. There was a lot of commotion in the camp, and people came to check out the new arrivals. As Ephriam and his brothers were setting up their tents, some older girls walked past several times, giggling as they checked out the three young men putting up the tents.

Seaton, who was helping his mother build a fire so she could cook supper, whistled at some of the girls that passed by, ignoring the bops from a wooden spoon wielded by his mother. A couple of girls were bold enough to stop and chat.

A chubby blond sidled up to Cam, pointed at him, and said in her distinctive Oklahoma accent, "You're gonna be the lucky guy who gets to take me to the dance Saturday night."

Cam gave a sheepish grin, and his brothers laughed. Even their usually stoic mother grinned.

Ephriam rescued Cam from his embarrassment.

"Where is this dance going to be that my brother here is taking you to?"

"Did you see that park about a half mile down the road? Well, it's right there in that ol' white building that's called the community hall."

Cam gave the girl a once over while Ephriam talked to her. She wasn't a bad looking girl, but dark red lipstick covered her dirty teeth, and it revolted him.

"I can't dance worth a hoot; you don't want to do any dancing with me. Ephriam here is the dancer—he loves to dance."

The teeth didn't get by Ephriam either, who shot a 'you're going to be sorry' look over at his brother.

"I want you, not your brother, and I'll teach y'all to dance. I'm very good, ain't I, Mary Ellen?"

She turned to the small brunette standing beside her, whose pixie face was overwhelmed by huge brown eyes.

The girl lowered her eyelids and spoke softly in the same accent as her friend. "She really is good; she's always teaching people to dance."

Cam shook his head. "I don't think we'll be able to go to the dance; we all have too much to do."

"Oh, I think we might be able to make it," Ephriam said, "but on one condition—that your friend here will go with me."

"Sure she will. Won't you, Mary Ellen?"

"I reckon so." She lowered her eyes again.

"What's your name?" the blonde asked. "Mine's Estalee Crowder." She put her hand out to Cam. Cam took it unwillingly and said nothing.

"He's Cam. I'm Ephriam, and that guy pounding those stakes is Harrison."

"Who's this cutie-pie here?" Estalee asked, referring to Seaton. Seaton still wore the huge grin that he had pasted on since coming to join his brothers.

"Did you forget to put your eye glasses on? That ugly bug is Seaton," Ephriam said.

"I know just the gal for ol' Seaton. Shirley Ann, my twelve-year-old sister. He'll love her. She's as cute as a button."

"That boy ain't going nowhere," Fairzina said. She then ordered Seaton to get back over and put wood on the fire.

Oregon

Estalee lowered her voice as she said, "I'm sure my cousin Bertie would love to go with Harrison. Don't worry," she called to Harrison, "She's real cute, and everyone says she looks just like me."

Cam wasn't happy about Ephriam setting him up, and this made for a lot of contention between the two brothers for the rest of that day; it ended only when Ephriam agreed to go see Estalee the next morning and tell her that Cam wasn't feeling all that great and wouldn't be able to go to the dance.

This news didn't upset Estalee; she just told Ephriam that it was his lucky day, because he would be taking two beautiful girls instead of one. Ephriam, caught in his own trap, started thinking up ways to avoid having to get close to Estalee.

On his way back from Estalee's, Ephriam passed a camp where a girl and an older woman were sitting by a fire. They were both very pretty with dark brown hair, blue eyes, and delicate features, but their faces were covered with a profound sadness. For the rest of the day, those faces haunted Ephriam, especially the girl's. He walked past their camp two more times that afternoon, but no one was around, and he didn't hear anyone stirring inside the tent. He hoped the girl would be at the dance, and he wished he had stopped that morning to become acquainted with them.

On Saturday, Ephriam and Harrison walked to the dance with the girls they agreed to accompany. Cam didn't go with them but did show up about two hours later. When Estalee saw him, she put her hands on her hips, gave a harrumph, and stuck her nose in the air. She continued to do this between bouts of dancing with a couple of her cousins.

Cam didn't like the way that Estalee's cousins looked at him. He told Ephriam this and said that he was going to walk back to camp.

A couple of minutes after Cam left, Ephriam noticed that Estalee's cousins weren't in the hall. He got an uneasy feeling and went outside to see if they were around. As soon as he got outside, he heard scuffling noises coming from the road, and he could make out forms thrashing about.

He ran toward them and found that Estalee's cousins had Cam on the ground and were pummeling him with punches. Ephriam grabbed them both around the neck and squeezing as hard as he could, he pulled them off Cam. They sputtered, coughed and tried to pry his arms off, but he held on with all his might. Cam stumbled up and gave each a couple of hard punches to the gut.

"You guys had enough?" Ephriam asked, tightening his hold.

"Yeah, yeah," one of them squeaked.

Ephriam released his hold on them, and they took off trotting toward camp.

"Are you okay?" Ephriam asked Cam.

"I guess so, but my face hurts like hell."

When they got back to the campfire, Ephriam saw that Cam's face was covered with blood.

"Damn, Cam, you're messed up, you better go to the pump over there and wash up."

He kept his voice low so his folks would not hear. He didn't want their mother to see Cam like that. She would never let them hear the end of it. She gave them hell whenever they even got into a scuffle amongst themselves and would tan their hides real good if they got into a fight with anyone else. Even though their father was known as a gentle man, his outlook about fighting differed from his wife's. He would tell his boys to avoid it any way they could, but he had come to blows a few times himself when some jerk couldn't keep his mouth shut.

One of those times was when Early Evens and Josh Talbot—ne'er-do-well heathens that looked as though they had fallen off the dump wagon—came into the reverend's church in Virginia, like they had done a couple of times before, just to aggravate the regular parishioners. Reverend Campbell had already warned them twice not to come back, but they didn't heed his warnings.

That Sunday had been special for the little church, a young couple was getting married, and there would be a potluck and music. Everyone looked forward to having a great time.

The women were setting up the table, and the reverend was helping carry the food to the table. As he looked for a spot to set the platter of fried chicken, someone came up behind him. From the smell, he knew who it was.

"I hope y'all don't mind if me and ol' Josh take in this-here weddin'. We ain't got no place else to go this swell afternoon."

Reverend Campbell turned slightly and faced Early's sickening, snaggletooth grin, got the full force of his putrid breath, and then turned back to what he was doing.

"I don't think that is a good idea. You weren't invited," the reverend said, looking for a place to set the platter. Early, who was as dim as a lantern without a wick, nudged the reverend's arm hard enough to knock the platter from his hands, sending it into the wedding cake. And then he reacted in the dumbest way possible—he laughed.

This made the reverend's blood boil. He had his fill of the

overgrown goof and sent his elbow into his gut as hard as he could. It knocked the breath out of Early, who crumpled to his knees. Josh just stood looking at him with his mouth open.

Reverend Campbell turned slowly, and said to Josh, "You get that scoundrel and get out of here while you're able to, and I'd better not see you here again."

"Yes, sir," Josh said as he grabbed his pathetic pal by both arms and pulled him out of sight.

There was never another incident with those two, but there were relatives of Early's who tried to start trouble with the reverend and his boys, but afterwards were sorry they tried, because it always ended in a very painful way for them. Before long, word got around that you better not fool with Reverend Campbell, and after those incidents, he never had to resort to fisticuffs with anyone.

Cam washed up and went to bed, and Ephriam went back to the dance to explain to Mary Ellen why he had disappeared. He arrived at the hall to find Mary Ellen standing against a wall, looking forlorn. When he went up to her, she didn't look at him.

"Hey, Mary Ellen, I'm sorry I had to leave, but when I went outside to see about Cam, he wasn't feeling too good, so I walked him back to camp."

Mary Ellen didn't respond.

"Come on, let's dance," Ephriam said. He grabbed her hand and pulled her onto the floor.

Estalee interrupted their dancing. "Do you guys know where those two dumb cousins of mine went?"

"Didn't they leave?" Ephriam asked.

"Yeah, but they said they would come right back after they took care of something."

"You know those idiots, Estee, they're probably drunk on their butts somewhere," Mary Ellen said.

"Yeah, I reckon so," Estalee said and turned to Ephriam. "Hey, you owe me at least one dance." She pushed Mary Ellen aside and took his hands.

"I was just telling Mary Ellen that I'm not feeling so good; I think I better get going," Ephriam said, trying to avoid being close to the repulsive girl.

"Throw up on me, I don't care, but you're going to dance with me before you leave," Estalee said as she pressed herself close to him and started moving.

"Jesus," Ephriam said, looking at Mary Ellen, who shrugged and left for the wall.

Luckily for Ephriam, the music ended shortly after, and he went to join Mary Ellen.

Estalee followed him. "Hey y'all, let's go to the park and hang out."

She bellowed over to Harrison and Bertie, who were waiting for the next dance. "Get over here."

They came over and Harrison, Bertie, Estalee, and Mary Ellen decided to go the park. Ephriam had had enough of Estalee for one night.

"I'm going back to camp," Ephriam said. "You guys don't have too much fun now."

Ephriam returned to camp, thinking about the girl with the sad eyes that he had seen earlier that day.

The next day, the family went exploring around Hood River. Reverend Campbell said that he liked the area, and hoped he could get a church there. The rest of the family said they agreed with him and wouldn't mind at all if they were to settle there.

It was dark when they arrived back at the camp. They all turned in early because the hops would be starting the next morning, and they had to get up at daybreak.

The Barkers were among the first in the vineyard. After getting their sacks and selecting their rows, they all donned their hats and gloves and began stripping the hops from the vine. They worked as fast as they could; they wanted to get the hops in the sacks while they were still wet with dew. They were paid by the pound so it was important to finish before it warmed up and the water dissipated.

But Ephriam couldn't concentrate very well that morning; he spent a lot of time looking around at the other workers. He was looking for the girl with the sad eyes, and he finally spotted her working several rows away.

Ephriam couldn't keep his eyes off the girl, but couldn't get up enough courage to go over and talk to her.

"Ephriam, what are you staring at?" Cam asked. "Go over and talk to her. You're not doing any work anyway."

"Mind your own business. I'm working harder than you are."

Cam called to Earl, who was working with their mother. "Come here a minute."

Earl ran to him. Cam whispered into Earl's ear. "Go over to that girl and tell her that Ephriam loves her."

Earl grinned and ran over to the girl.

Ephriam spotted Earl talking with the girl and knew immediately that Cam had put him up to it. He was about to tear into Cam, when Earl came running up, grinning.

"Ephriam, that girl over there says she loves you, too."

Ephriam bopped him on the head and said, "You had no business talking to that girl, and you better not go near her again!"

Earl rubbed his head. "Now I'm not gonna tell you what she really said."

"I think you will, if you know what's good for you." Ephriam made a gesture that he was going to bop him again.

Earl drew back. "Her name is **Mary**, and she's fifteen years old."

He hesitated a moment, then continued. "But she said you're as ugly as a mud fence, and she doesn't want to know you." He took off running before he got the last word out.

"Well, Ephriam, When are you gonna go introduce yourself?" Harrison asked.

"Maybe I'm not," Ephriam said

"If you don't, I am," Harrison said.

"Don't even think about it." Ephriam narrowed his eyes at him.

At the close of the second day of work, Ephriam went up to the girl and introduced himself. As he walked her back to her camp, he found out that Mary and her family were still mourning the death of her brother **Joseph**, who had drowned just a month before while swimming in the Columbia River near their home in Lyle, Washington. The family was heartbroken at losing the loving sixteen-year-old, who had saved them from starvation many times with the squirrels, birds and rabbits he hunted.

In the days that followed, Ephriam spent most of his free time with Mary and her family. He tried his best to cheer them up and was able to get them to laugh a little more each day. He especially liked to talk with Mary's mother, **Margaret McWilliams**, who had an Irish brogue and a melodious laugh that lit up her sorrowful eyes. He liked her father, **Chauncey Peterman**, as well; a pleasant man quite knowledgeable on almost any subject discussed. And he enjoyed Mary's four siblings: **Madge**, a shy twelve-year-old, **John**, a curious eleven-year-old, seven-year-old **David**, and two-year-old **Frank**.

Every evening after work was finished, Ephriam and Mary took a walk through the park. They would sit on a bench and talk until it was almost dark. Only two weeks after meeting Mary, Ephriam knew he had found the girl he wanted to marry.

On the eve of the last day of hops, Ephriam decided it was time to tell Mary how he felt about her. He chose the spot that she liked best in the park—a huge cork tree that had a perfect grassy spot for sitting.

Mary looked pretty in her brown cotton dress. Her shiny dark brown hair was rolled into a bun, as she always wore it, and the sadness that had been in her eyes was now almost gone.

Ephriam loved the sweetness that was so much a part of her. He had watched her with her family, and there was such tenderness in her relationships with all of them. She was so helpful with her siblings, and never said a cross word to any of them.

That evening, as they sat under that huge cork tree, he took her hand. "Mary, I need to tell you something, and I hope I'm not going to scare you."

Ephriam Buck Barker

She laughed nervously. "I hope it's nothing too serious. I've had too much seriousness lately."

"No, this is good. I know we haven't known each other very long, but in this short time, I have come to care very deeply for you, and I want you to be my wife."

Mary didn't answer right away, so Ephriam continued. "I realize that you are not of age yet, but I am hoping there will be some way that we can arrange it."

Mary picked up a twig and drew a heart in the dirt. She put her initials inside it and put Ephriam's underneath hers.

"Even if we could get married, somehow, I don't think my folks would let me."

Ephriam took her face in his hands. "We can do this; just let me take care of everything. I'll talk to your folks, and I'll make this happen."

That evening, Ephriam told Mary's family that he wanted to marry her as soon as possible. But the reaction of Mary's mother put a damper on what Ephriam hoped would be welcomed news.

"'Tis what you want to do with me Mary?" Margaret asked.

"Maggie, give the boy a chance to present himself," Chauncey said and motioned Ephriam to come sit beside him.

"Ephriam, you know that Mary is only fifteen, so I am assuming that you are talking about doing this after she turns sixteen."

"I want to marry her now, and I think it will a good thing for all of us. You and Margaret are trying to build a life together again, and it will be easier if you know that Mary has someone to take care of her."

Margaret straightened up to the limit that her five-feet-two inches would reach.

"Hold on, me lad, I've no thing against ye, but me Mary is not going to become a wife at this young age."

"Mama, I want to marry Ephriam, and I think it would be better if we do it right away," Mary said, coming to stand beside Ephriam.

"'Tisn't going to happen, girl," Margaret said.

They bantered for about an hour before Ephriam thought he'd better drop the subject until another time.

After Ephriam left, Margaret took Mary into the tent. They sat on a mattress that was on the ground. It was covered with a faded blue wool blanket full of holes.

"Mary, me girl, I shan't let ye end up having to live the rest

of your life going from tent to tent with nothing but hunger and dirt floors to look forward to. 'Tis a terrible life, and ye have plenty of time to meet a fine gentleman who will give ye a good life."

"But you don't know that for sure, Mama, and no one can guarantee what will happen in the future. I want to do this," Mary said as tears eased from her eyes.

"Aw, now, Mary, I know how ye feel. I felt that way once, meself." Margaret shook her head as she ran her fingers over the holes in the worn blanket. "'Tisn't enough to make a marriage. Ye don't want to end up having to let your children go to someone else because ye can't take care of their needs. Believe this Mary, 'tisn't a thing worse in God's world then watching your babes go hungry."

"That will never happen to me. I'll never, ever, let my children go away from me. Mama, I know that you did the best you could, and I don't blame you for us being separated. I only meant that I don't think Ephriam would ever go away and leave his family like Father did. I know he wouldn't."

"I will be praying for ye, my child; 'tis all I can do. But, please, Mary, ye shouldn't do this right away. Please wait just a few more months. "

"Mama, waiting won't change the way I feel."

Margaret McWilliams & brother Patrick

Margaret McWilliams knew the consequences that could come from marrying too young. She had done that herself shortly after arriving from Ireland. She married Chauncey Peterman and soon after, found her life fraught with hardships.

Chauncey went off for long periods leaving her with the children to care for without any help from him or anyone.

One of those times, she was left on the prairie in South Dakota, and she did laundry for the miners, working her fingers raw. It was meager pay, and she was lucky to have had chickens to trade with the Sioux Indians for corn and other foods. She did all she could to take care of the children, but it was just too difficult to keep them fed and clothed, and she had to eventually let some of them go to other places for their care.

Mary & Joseph Peterman

Besides having to place Mary, Joseph, and Madge in St. James Orphanage in Benson, Nebraska, she let the two youngest children, **Elizabeth** and **James**, go to live with her sister **Della**, who had come from Ireland with her. This was supposed to have been a temporary arrangement but it didn't turn out that way—Della refused to give the children back. Margaret would never see those two children again. There were two other boys, John and David, who she was able to keep with her.

After Margaret moved to Lyle, Chauncey moved back in and began working as a carpenter while Margaret took in boarders. She began saving pennies and nickels until she had enough for the train fare to bring her three children home. She sent for Joseph and Madge first, and saved again until she had enough to bring Mary home. By 1911 she had all three back with her. She also gave birth to **Francis (Frank)** in 1910.

Mary & Ephriam Barker

Margaret tried to prevent her daughter from marrying Ephriam, but Chauncey forged a document saying Mary was sixteen, and Ephriam's father, Reverend Campbell, married them on September 14, 1913, in Mission Bottoms at the site of the Old Catholic Mission.

Ephriam's sister Lillie was also married at that time to Noel Reed.

Ephriam and Mary remained in that area for a short while after their marriage then followed Ephriam's parents and Mary's family to Birmingham, Washington.

Oregon

It was there that the alcohol Ephriam was so fond of began causing problems. The drinking bouts with his brother Harrison were all the more frequent now.

Mary hated his drinking and there were a few times when he did try to quit, but they didn't last very long.

When Mary became pregnant with their first child, he promised that he had taken his last drink, and Mary wanted desperately to believe him.

Ephriam kept his promise for a few weeks before starting to drink again. And when he did, he would stop before getting drunk. Things were better when their first child, **August Leonard**, was born on August 20, 1914.

Soon after the birth, Ephriam decided that they should go to California. Mary wasn't happy about that; she didn't want to leave her mother after being separated from her for so many years, and it would break her mother's heart.

Margaret had been through so much heartache the past year. Soon after Ephriam and Mary's wedding, Chauncey left again, leaving her with their six children. And to make things worse, after being gone a few months, he sent her a letter begging her to give him another chance. Margaret was all too eager to do that, as she always was, but a few days before his expected return, she received another letter from him. He wrote that he was sorry, but after thinking it over, he didn't think reconciling was a good idea and that he thought they should get a divorce. The letter devastated Margaret, and she grieved as if he had died. She later learned that while she was waiting for his return, he had met another woman and wanted to marry her.

Mary put off telling her mother about their leaving until the day before they were to go.

They were having their usual Sunday supper at Margaret's house, and Mary decided to tell her when they were alone in the kitchen.

Mary dried the supper dishes and tried to think of the best way to break the news, when her mother interrupted her thoughts.

"How shall we celebrate the wee lad's first birthday?" 'Tis only two weeks from now, ye know. Why don't we have the celebration here? I'll make the cake."

Mary felt a lump rise in her throat and could barely get the words out, "Mama, we won't be here on August's birthday. We're leaving for California tomorrow morning."

Margaret let the piece of firewood she was picking up fall back into the woodbin. She turned and looked at Mary with the same expression in her eyes that she always got when fear overtook her.

"Sakes, girl, ye gave me a fright. Sounded like ye said ye were leaving." She was shaking her head as she turned to pick up the wood again.

Mary went to her mother, took the wood from her, and put it into the fire.

"Mama, I did say we were leaving."

Margaret returned to her dishpan and continued washing dishes.

"Look at ye, now, Mary mine, ye are saying things that I shan't believe."

Mary stepped behind her mother and put her arms around her.

"I don't want to leave, but Ephriam says that we can do better in California. He'll be able to get a steady job."

"Ye will be going out of my life again, on to something that may not be good. Ye've not been happy for a long time now, and 'tis just what I expected."

"Mama, please don't say anything like that to Ephriam. Promise me you won't."

But that was one promise that Margaret couldn't make, and she went outside where Ephriam and her children were playing with August.

Mary followed her, plucked August up, and went back into the house. She didn't want to hear what was going to be said.

Margaret stood in front of Ephriam and put her hands on her hips.

"Well, me lad, what is this nonsense about ye taking me girl from me? Aye, and the wee one, too?"

"Maggie, I have to do what's best for my family, and I'm not taking your girl away for good. I'll make sure we come back here often to see you. Maybe you should come to California, too."

"Ephriam, 'tisn't possible to traipse around after ye. Stay here. There are jobs here that a lad can make money at. And what about your folks? How can ye go gallivanting off and leave them behind?"

Ephriam had hoped his family wouldn't be mentioned.

"My folks are coming with us, Maggie, and I wish you could come, too."

Margaret just shook her head and went inside.

Ephriam felt bad as he watched her walk away. That look of sadness that had been in Margaret's eyes when he first met her had returned, and he had caused it.

They left soon after that, with Margaret standing on the porch waving gently as they drove off. Mary cried as she watched her mother.

Oregon

Somehow, deep down she knew it would be the last time she would see her.

Tragedy in California

Ephriam settled his family in Eureka, California, and his parents and brothers settled close by. There, on Oct. 31, 1916, Mary gave birth to **Elden Ephriam**.

August & Elden "Bud"

From there, they went to Marysville where **Ruth Mary** was born on June 6, 1918, and on Sept. 30, 1919, **Earl Clifton** was born in Oroville. On December 10, 1920, Mary gave birth to **Edith Viola** at Pentz.

Tragedy in California

While living in Oroville, Ephriam's brother Earl died from consumption on March 21, 1921. He was twenty-one years old.

In April of 1921, Ephriam moved his family to Hilton, California, and it was there that the worst tragedy of their lives happened.

On Christmas Day 1921, Mary was preparing dinner when three-year-old Ruthie came to her and said her head hurt. Mary had noticed earlier that she looked flushed but thought it was because she was standing near the wood range that was going full force. She put her hand on Ruthie's forehead. She was burning up with fever. Mary sponged Ruthie's face with cool water and gave her an aspirin.

Mary was stricken with fear, as she always was when her children were sick. She agonized over the thought that it could be one of those deadly diseases that often ended in death.

Mary's stomach was in knots. She couldn't eat any of the dinner she prepared. Ruthie only took a couple of bites of her meal before wanting to lie down. During dinner, seven-year-old August complained of a headache and sore throat. Mary gave him an aspirin, and he went to her old rocking chair, as he often did when he wasn't feeling well.

Ruthie began having bouts of vomiting, and August, who was always more concerned for others than he was for himself, motioned his mother to him.

Not wanting Ruthie to hear his concerns, he whispered, "Mama, I'm worried about Ruthie. She's so sick, is there anything we can do to make her feel better?"

Mary was in awe of the green-eyed little man who never ceased to amaze everyone with empathy and wisdom far beyond his years.

"I can read a story to her. That always seems to make her feel better. It'll make you feel better too. Come, lie down with her, and I'll get the Snow White storybook."

Ruth vomited all night, and her fever raged. August tried to be so brave, and although he was as sick as Ruthie, he told his mother he was feeling better. But Mary knew better. She saw the tears that filled his eyes when he thought she wasn't looking.

It was a terrible night. The sick children kept the other three children — five-year-old Bud, two-year-old Earl, and one-year-old Edith, awake most of the night, and Mary and Ephriam had to comfort them, as well as tend to August and Ruth.

The next day, a doctor was summoned, and Mary's worst fear was realized — it was typhoid fever.

The hell they went through that holiday season, with caring for the children who became sicker with each passing day and worrying that the others would become sick, was a time so horrendous that nothing could ease their pain.

The first three days of the children's sickness, Ephriam came home sober, but on the fourth day, his old habit was back. After work, he would stop by his parents' house, and he and Harrison would go out to the barn where Harrison kept the booze stashed. Ephriam didn't stay long. He quickly downed enough booze to get a mild buzz and then would rush home.

One day, he seemed sober when he first got home, but every half hour or so, he went out to his car and stayed for about five minutes, drinking from a bottle he had stashed there.

That evening, Mary tried to feed the sick children and get some water down them, but it was no use. Ruth vomited immediately after drinking some water, and August forced himself to eat some chicken soup but couldn't keep it down.

Mary was on her hands and knees cleaning up the vomit when Ephriam came in from a round of car sitting.

"What happened here?" he asked.

Mary burst into tears. Her nerves were shot, and she had nothing but resentment for the man standing over her. She completely broke down and sobbed so hard that little Bud came running to her. He slipped on the slime, but Mary caught him and held him so tightly that he started to cough.

Ephriam pried Bud from her arms then helped her off the floor and held her close to him.

"Mary, I'm sorry." He led her to a chair and then knelt before her. He put his head in her lap and said, his voice breaking, "Mary, I tried not to drink, but I'm so afraid of what might happen to our kids."

"Ephriam, you find any reason to drink, even though you know it makes things worse for all of us."

After putting Bud, Earl, and Edith to bed, the two sat by the bedside of their sick children, staring at the only lights in the room: the blue and red Christmas lights on the little tree that August helped his father cut a few days before he became ill. He had taken such pride in picking it out and had been filled with joy when helping to decorate it.

He had even made his mother a wreath from the branches that were cut from the bottom of the tree. He put pinecones on it and made a ribbon from a piece of old gunnysack.

That night, in that surreal setting, Ephriam once more made a vow to Mary that he would stop drinking.

Mary's strength weakened with each passing day, and although she tried hard to stay awake to care for her children, exhaustion would overtake her, and she would drift off to sleep.

There was another reason Mary didn't want to sleep: she often had dreams and visions that were prophetic, and she couldn't bear to have one of those now.

But what she feared did happen early one morning as she sat at the bedside of her sick children. She had closed her eyes for a few seconds and when she opened them again, she saw an angel sitting at the foot of the bed.

Mary knew that the apparition meant that there would be a death soon, and a cold, numbing chill ran through her, almost paralyzing her.

Two days after Mary's dream, on the evening of January 4, 1922, Ruth stopped breathing. The doctor was there at the time and after he told Ephriam that she had died, the distraught father picked up his baby girl and cradled her in his arms. With his face ashen, he rocked her, smoothing back the golden-brown curls that framed her angelic face. He remembered the day she was born; she was so beautiful and delicate. He worshiped her and didn't know how he could go on without her.

In shock, Mary hadn't moved at all since Dr. Folsom told them Ruth was dead. She sat at the foot of August's bed, staring at her boy. The tremendous ache in her throat crushed her. She could barely breathe, and if it weren't for the other children, she would have gladly succumbed to its desire to snuff the life out of her. For the first time in her life, she questioned God. Why couldn't he have healed her children? She had prayed so hard. She wanted her mother, and she needed her like no other time in her life.

Before leaving to arrange for Ruthie's body to be taken from the house to be prepared for burial, the doctor convinced Ephriam that it was time to let his little girl go. Reluctantly, he laid her on the bed that he and Mary slept in and covered her with the blanket Mary had made for her when she was born. He kissed his baby girl's cheek for the last time and then hurried out the door, trying to hold back the sobs that burst out as soon as he was outside.

Ephriam went to his parents' place. He told them he could not bear to go back home until his little girl's body was removed from the house, so he stayed with Harrison while his parents went to be with Mary.

Harrison said they would follow in a few minutes, but after an hour had passed and they had not arrived, Reverend Campbell went to see why. As he pulled into his driveway, his two sons came out of the barn, and Ephriam had trouble walking. With the help of Harrison, Campbell put Ephriam in his car, and they took him home. They helped him into the house and laid him on his bed. Finding Ruthie's blanket laying beside him, the grieving father buried his face in it, and sobs racked his body.

Fairzina made coffee, and they all sat in silence as they watched little Edith sit on the floor and play with some empty thread spools that Mary had strung together. She was smiling with the innocence of a one-year-old.

Bud and Earl sat in the rocking chair, and Earl had fallen asleep. Bud held his hand and tried hard to be still so he wouldn't wake him. Bud was sad. He was old enough to feel the effects of such a tragedy. He adored his little sister, and she felt the same about him. He was so helpful and patient with her, and she had shown her appreciation by planting little kisses on him.

After some prayers over August, Ephriam's family left. They offered to take the children who were not sick home with them, but Mary didn't want them out of her sight. She had to have them near because seeing that they were still healthy was the only thing that kept her from breaking down.

Ephriam stayed home from work for a few days following Ruthie's death, and he and Mary took turns sitting with August during the night. They were like zombies—a heavy, vague feeling had taken over their minds and bodies, dulling their pain some.

A week after Ruth died, after having the worst night of his illness, August awoke and smiled feebly up at his mother sitting at his side. He told her that he had something to tell her.

His voice was weak, and Mary lay down beside him so she could hear what he had to say. She took his hand and put it to her cheek.

"Mama, I had the most beautiful dream. I'm going to tell you about it, but I don't want you to be worried when I do."

Fear washed over her. She had a feeling that her little boy's dream was one she didn't want to hear. The urge to cry overwhelmed her, but she summoned up every ounce of her will and vowed to hold the tears back.

"Please tell me your beautiful dream, August."

"I was in this beautiful place, and I wasn't sick anymore. I was feeling so good, the way I used to feel, and when I got there, Ruthie was waiting for me. She looked so pretty, just like you, Mama, and she wasn't sick anymore either. She was laughing and so happy to see me. And when I saw her, I knew that someday you and Papa and everybody we love would be there with us."

Tragedy in California

Mary broke the vow she made to herself and the tears flooded out.

"Mama, it'll be okay. I feel much better now. Doesn't that make you happy, Mama?"

Mary dried her tears on her apron, kissed August's cheek, and forced a smile. "That makes me very happy."

August then asked his mother to sing the hymns that he loved, and she had to turn her head while singing so he wouldn't see the tears that were flowing again.

August died the next day on January 12, 1922.

The other children didn't contract the disease.

Three months after the deaths of her two children, on April 10, 1922, Mary gave birth to **John David**. The children kept her very busy, but the painful reminder of the house being the place where her children had died kept Mary in such a state of sadness that she could barely function. Ephriam wanted to move to another house soon after August died, but Mary didn't want to move. She could feel the spirits of their dead children in the house. But after a while, her sadness affected the children.

After August's death, she had left the wreath he had made for her hanging on the door where he had put it. One day, Bud got a chair, climbed up, and started to take the wreath down. When Mary saw what he was doing, she grabbed him, tripped over the chair, and sent them both to the floor.

Bud was scared more than hurt, and he bawled at the top of his voice. He put his arms around his mother. Mary realized how she must have scared him. She had reacted too quickly and in the wrong way. But just seeing the wreath off the door where August had placed it instantly angered her. This was something new to her. She had never overreacted like that before.

She held her sobbing little boy in her arms and comforted him. "Mama's sorry."

Bud pulled back, wiped his eyes, and said, lisping, "I only wanted to wrap it up so I could give it to you. We were playing Christmas, and I was pretending I was August, so I wanted to give you the wreath."

That broke Mary's heart. She looked at Earl, and little Edith, who was just a toddler, and saw the frightened looks on their little faces. She realized that she had not fully understood how much Bud was grieving and that the game was a way for him to deal with his grief.

She got up, put the chair back at the table, and announced to the children, "I want to play Christmas with you. That sounds like fun. Bud, you go ahead and wrap the wreath, and I'll help all of you wrap presents for each other. We'll wrap one for Papa, too. He'll be happy that we're having Christmas again."

She gave them some brown paper bags to use as wrapping paper and some red yarn to use as ties. She told them to go outside and find things they could use to make presents, like pretty rocks, leaves, twigs, or anything that could be wrapped.

When Bud and Earl came in from their gleaning, Earl was holding a baby frog. It looked like the life had been squished out of the poor little thing.

"We can't wrap a frog," Mary said.

Earl began to cry.

"We could put it in a jar with a little water and leaves," Bud said.

Mary took the frog and examined it. Maybe it would be all right after all. Bud got the jar ready, and Earl placed the frog in it, grinning as he did. Bud and his mother exchanged smiles, seeing the happiness on the little guy's face.

They spent the rest of the afternoon wrapping their presents. Mary felt joy for the first time since the deaths, and after that day, she tried to spend some time each day playing with her little ones.

Three months later, they moved to Yuba City, and Ephriam went to work for the county, doing roadwork. The pain from the deaths of the children had lessened, and he was trying to keep his promise of not drinking, but sometimes, the temptation was just too great, especially when he was with Harrison, who always managed to get liquor somehow.

It was here that Mary gave birth to **Robert (Bobby) Granville** on May 25, 1923.

Mary liked the area around Yuba City. It reminded her of where she lived as a child in South Dakota, and it made her miss her mother more than ever.

She often talked to Ephriam about going for a visit, but he always told her the same thing, that as soon as they could get some extra money, they would do that. But with every passing year, she knew it wasn't going to happen.

Mary had wondered many times what her life would have been like if she hadn't been raised in the convent, and hadn't been taught that it was a sin to do anything to prevent a pregnancy or to deny your husband's needs, no matter what the consequences.

She never had discussions with anyone about marriage and children. At the convent, she had learned the strict rules her religion had about those things, and they were not up for questioning. After she had returned home, she attempted to speak with her mother, but somehow it always seemed that the time wasn't right. Besides, her mother, like all of her Irish grandmothers, had deep-rooted beliefs and often told her children that they should never go against their religion. She told them that their roles in this life had been cast and that they had to play them out to the end, no matter what life handed them.

Mary accepted this, but her longing to see her mother never lessened. And although she spent many nights crying herself to sleep, when morning came, she always felt better. She would start singing as soon as she rose. It would lift her spirits, and then she would be able to greet her family with a smile.

Mary's mother passed away in 1937 at age 62 without seeing her oldest daughter for more than twenty years. Mary wasn't able to go to her funeral at Hood River, Oregon, and she had to grieve for her beloved mother without the comfort of her brothers, sisters and father.

Mary hadn't seen her father since that day in Birmingham, and it would be several years before she would see him again. Her sister Madge kept in touch with Mary as much as she possibly could, and would come to visit whenever she was able to locate her.

From Valley to Mountains

The family moved to Dos Palos, California in 1924 and was living in a large house, which Mary loved. It was the biggest one they had ever lived in, and there was a huge yard for the children to play in. They lived close to the school, and it would only take Earl and Bud a few minutes to walk there.

Ephriam's parents and Harrison lived a few miles down the road. The two families stuck close to one another, one moving when the other did. Harrison, who never married, lived with his parents most of the time.

Mary was glad that Ephriam's parents lived nearby. Ephriam was gone a lot, and she had to rely on them for many things. She was especially thankful that they were close by on January 13, 1925, when she needed a ride to the hospital for the birth of **Theodore (Teddy)**.

That winter, Ephriam trapped mink, raccoon and skunk with Harrison and his father. The skunks lived in dens not too far underground, so they were easy to get to. They would get three to ten skunks from each den. Most wild pelts brought a very good price at that time, so they were able to make a decent living out of trapping. Ephriam sold most of his furs green (with flesh) to Bill Burman in Sacramento, but he removed the flesh from the mink he shipped to M. Lyons, in Kansas City, Missouri.

The winter of 1925 was the best in a long time, and since Ephriam and Harrison were with their father most of the time, they didn't have a chance to drink as much.

When spring came, Ephriam and Harrison hunted coyote pups for the bounty. They dug out the dens, took the pups, skinned them, and took the pelts to a county that would pay the most for them. They used

Ephriam's Airedale dogs to ferret out raccoons. Sometimes Ephriam brought a coon carcass home for supper, and Mary would bake it.

After selling furs one day, a guy offered Ephriam a good deal on an old touring car. It was black and shiny and had screw knobs on each side of the windshield so it could be opened for air. During skunk season, he ran a wire through the nose of the pelts, about twenty in a bunch, and hung them, fur side out, on those knobs. A lot of people commented that it was a beautiful sight, the black pelts with white stripes hanging on both sides of that car.

In the spring of 1926, the family was at Yountville in the Napa Valley, and that's where **Patrick (Pat) Henry** was born on March 24.

Here, Ephriam and Harrison went to work as agents for the Pinkerton Detective Agency. They would go to the grape farmers that were bootlegging, buy whatever booze they were making, and take it to headquarters. The government would take over from that point. They also investigated any person suspected of bootlegging and destroyed any stills that were found. This was dangerous work.

That Old Demon Booze

Around the middle of June, the two received orders to investigate a place that was on a hill behind one of the more prosperous vineyards. They set out at daybreak, hoping there would be no one around the area. They parked their car in a grove of trees to camouflage it and proceeded up the hill, being as quiet as they could and listening to every sound as they went. They had been climbing the steep hill for several minutes and were almost to the top when a shot rang out. Ephriam felt a bullet whiz by his head. They both dropped to the ground as another shot tore through the air.

"What the hell do we do now?" Harrison asked Ephriam.

"We have to get out of here. Just scoot backward to the bottom, and we'll try to come up another way."

"Like hell," Harrison said. "I'm not going to get killed over somebody's stupid still."

"There's a smart man." A woman's voice, coming from behind them, startled Ephriam and Harrison.

They turned to face the barrel of a shotgun held by a small woman dressed in men's clothing several sizes too large. The clothes were old and faded, but they were clean. She was pretty, with chiseled features and green eyes, but there was a hardness to her face.

The woman laughed heartily. "Surprised you, didn't I? What're you guys doing on my hill? Lucky I didn't shoot you dead. I have that right, you know."

Ephriam pulled himself up to a sitting position, but Harrison lay there, afraid to move.

"We're just scouting out a hunting place..." Ephriam said.

"You're a damned liar," the woman interrupted. "You came her hoping to steal somebody's booze."

"Do you mind if I stand up?" Ephriam asked.

"All right, but don't try anything funny," she said, hoisting her gun a little higher. "Now, answer my question. You are here to try and find booze, aren't you? You better tell me, or I'm going to blow a hole in you big enough for an elephant to jump through."

Apparently she didn't think they were agents, which was a good sign.

"Okay, we live over here in Yountville and hoped to find someone who could tell us how to set up our own still. Some guy told us that you were the one to see," Ephriam said.

"I bet it was that no good Rhino who told you that. I knew he couldn't be trusted. The weasel. Well, he was lying. I don't have any still up here. I just got my little cabin. That's all I got." The woman motioned Ephriam to sit down.

"Is Rhino your husband?" Ephriam asked, as he lowered himself down.

The woman gave another hearty laugh. "Are you kidding? Would any woman marry that buzzard-bait?" She laughed again. "No way on God's green earth; that son-of-a-sick-bat did some work for me a few months back, and he was always snooping around. I had to run him off with this gun."

Ephriam tried a little polite charm. "By the way, I'm Ephriam Barker, and this is my brother, Harrison." He reached his hand out to her but she didn't take it.

She sat down and laid her gun across her lap, then said, "I'm Peggy Newman. She squinted her eyes. I'll tell you right now, I'm still suspicious of your reason for being here. I don't believe a damned thing any man says; they're all liars. Even Carson, my husband, was a liar. He couldn't tell the truth if his life depended on it, and as it turns out it did."

"Hey, look Peggy, I'm a family man, hell, I've got a dozen kids, and I'm not going to stick my neck out just to find a still to steal from. Harrison and I just want to find out how to build a still of our own. We haven't had a drink since we got here, and I really need something for my nerves. I recently lost two of my children, and sometimes the pain gets unbearable; I need something to soften it."

The green eyes softened as she said, "That's bad, real bad. I know how you feel. I lost my child before it could be born, and I can never have another."

The hardness returned to her eyes. "I still don't know if I should believe the reason you gave for being here. How do I know that you didn't come here to rape me, or do something else awful to me?"

"God, no. We wouldn't do that. Like I said, we just want to be able to have a drink or two when we want; we're not criminals or perverts," Ephriam said.

"Let's go, Ephriam. I don't think she knows anything about bootlegging," Harrison said.

He started to stand up, but Peggy jumped up and pushed him back down with the barrel of her gun.

"I haven't decided if I want you guys to leave or not." She stood looking at them for a minute. "Both of you get up and start walking up the hill."

Harrison looked at Ephriam with apprehension in his eyes.

"Come on, now, Peggy. I've got to get some food to take home to the kids. They'll be starving by now." Ephriam hoped this would make her relent.

"Just walk and keep quiet." She prodded Ephriam with her gun, and he started to walk. When they neared the top of the hill, a cabin came into view. It was small, but looked nice. The front porch was covered in climbing roses, and lace curtains showed through the windows. Barking came from inside, and it sounded like it came from a very large dog.

Peggy led them up the steps to where a bantam rooster was obliterating a corncob in front of the door. "Get out of the way, Dickens." She gently nudged him with her foot. "Now, I want to warn you about my dog; he won't bother you unless I tell him to, or unless you make a fast move, so when we get inside, I want you to sit down at the table, and stay there."

She opened the door, and sure enough, there was a huge, brown boxer waiting for them. Peggy went to him, petted him and told him to lie down, which he did.

"Silas Mack, meet Ephriam and Harrison." The giant dog gave a low growl but didn't move.

Peggy went to her cupboard and laid her gun against the wall next to it. She then got down three glasses and put them on the table. She went back to the cupboard again and brought back a large molasses bottle.

"Boys, maybe I should have been little more hospitable, so I'm going to share a little of my special drink with you."

"I always wanted to drink molasses from a crystal glass," Ephriam said, picking up a glass and examining it.

Everything in the cabin was of fine quality. A cabinet was filled with beautiful china, and a silver tea set was on top of the walnut buffet.

"You have a real nice home here, Peggy. How long have you been living in it?" Harrison asked.

"We built it ten years ago and moved into it as soon as it was done." She finished filling the glasses and then sat down.

Ephriam and Harrison both took a drink, after which Ephriam said, "This is the best molasses that I've ever tasted in my life. You're going to have to tell us how to get a hold of some like this."

Harrison nodded his head. "That's for damned sure. I wouldn't mind paying extra for this."

They emptied their glasses, and Peggy filled them again. They were all becoming more comfortable, and after a third round, they were beginning to feel pretty good.

The dog was sleeping, and that made Ephriam and Harrison feel a lot safer.

"Peggy, tell us about your husband and how you ended up here," Ephriam said.

"I guess I could tell you a little bit about that. About twelve years ago, only a few months after Carson and I were married, he got a letter from a lawyer here in Napa that said there was a possibility that Carson could be related to the people who owned Parrott Vineyards. Just before Dennis's father died, he confessed that he had gotten a young girl pregnant, and that she agreed to put the baby up for adoption. That letter threw Dennis for a loop; he never had any clue that he was adopted.

"There was a date set so the parties could meet and get acquainted with one another. We were living in Richmond, Virginia, at the time and..."

Ephriam interrupted. "You're kidding? We're from around that area. Were you born there?"

"I was born in a little hollow near Richmond, but Carson was born somewhere here in California, near San Francisco."

"This makes being here with you all the more special. Let's drink to that," Ephriam said. Peggy filled the glasses again, and they raised them in a toast.

"What did you do after the meeting was set up?" Harrison inquired.

"The lawyer sent us money for our train ticket, so we made a trip out here and went to the meeting. I tell you, when we first saw that grand house and those beautiful vineyards, we thought we must have been dreaming, especially on seeing the inside of the house. It was unbelievable.

"When the lawyer introduced us to the Parrotts, we were nervous, but they were cordial. Dennis did resemble Carson a bit; they had the same expressive gray eyes.

"We all talked for awhile and then had lunch. After lunch, the guys went off for a private discussion while Mrs. Parrott showed me around the vineyard. She didn't talk much, and she made me uneasy because she would eye me up every once in awhile. I got the idea that she didn't approve of me. I was very uncomfortable around her. She looked like a fashion model in her fancy clothes, and I had on a plain housedress.

"Anyways, it was decided that Carson and Dennis were brothers, and that we would move to the pretty house that sat behind the mansion and start becoming part of the business. We never really fit in, and Carson wasn't happy. He was so different than Dennis, and whether he just imagined it or not, he thought Dennis looked down on him.

"I loved our house, but after I lost my baby, everything just went downhill. Carson started arguing a lot with everyone. Finally his brother said he would give Carson the property that encompassed this hill, about forty acres, and that he could still work in the vineyard as long as he didn't cause any more trouble. Carson accepted. This was a lot better than being down there close to the mansion. We loved it up here on this hill. At least I thought Carson loved it as much as I did."

She tried to fill their glasses again, but the bottle was empty. She went to the cupboard and got another molasses bottle.

Ephriam was feeling a little woozy, but he wasn't going to refuse another drink. Harrison seemed to be holding up pretty well; he could always hold his liquor better than Ephriam. Peggy seemed to be doing all right.

After Peggy filled their glasses, she sat down and let out a huge sigh. "Well that's the boring story of how I come to be here."

Harrison let out a very loud sneeze. It startled Silas awake and he leaped up, started barking ferociously, and moved toward Harrison.

"Silas Mack! Get back!" Peggy commanded, and the dog eased

back to where he had been sleeping and flopped down.

"Jesus, I thought I was going to have a heart attack," Harrison said, patting his chest.

Ephriam felt that Peggy had left out the best part of her story; she had been hinting about problems with her husband, but didn't talk much about him.

"Peggy, tell us about Carson. Does he still live here with you?"

"Carson doesn't live anywhere. Carson doesn't live at all." Peggy was unsteady on her feet as she tried to get up, and fell back down in her chair.

Harrison jumped up and went to her. He put his arm around her. "Are you all right, Peggy?"

"Yeah, I'm fine; just got a little dizzy, that's all. I could use some water though."

Harrison took her empty glass and went to the sink.

Ephriam was concerned about Peggy, but he figured she just had too much to drink, and he really wanted to find out what happened to Carson. "Peggy, do you mean Carson is dead?"

Harrison looked at Ephriam and shook his head, but Ephriam continued, "Tell us what happened to him."

After drinking the water, Peggy closed her eyes and said, "You know, I'm not in the habit of talking to anyone about personal things that happened in my marriage."

She rubbed her eyes, and then glanced at Ephriam and Harrison. "But what the hell …you guys are my friends, aren't you?" She laid her hand on Ephriam's arm and began caressing it. "Sure you are; we were practically raised together, weren't we?" She winked at Harrison.

"That's right, and we're the best friends that you could ever find," Ephriam said, withdrawing his arm slowly away from the caressing hand.

"So you want to know what happened to Carson. Well, I'll tell you what happened to Carson; I killed him, that's what happened to him. I shot him dead."

Tears fell down her cheeks; she sat forward again, and there was anger in her voice as she said, "I killed the only man that I had ever cared about, and I did it with no more feeling than killing a cockroach."

She was sobbing now, and Harrison went to her again.

"Peggy, you don't have to say anymore." He glared at Ephriam.

Peggy sat up. "No, I want to talk about it; I need to talk about it. But I shouldn't be able to be here talking about it. I should be in prison."

She laid her head down on the table, let out a long sigh, then rose up, wiped the tears off her face and said, "It was his fault though, if he had only been truthful with me, I could have forgiven him anything. I gave him a chance to come clean with everything, but he only told more lies."

Peggy straightened herself up in her chair, and began telling them the events that led up to Carson's killing.

"When we first moved up here on the hill, everything seemed to go pretty good, but after a few months, Carson began to stay later and later at work and found every excuse he could to stay away from home. I was stuck up here on this hill and rarely went any place, so I begged Carson to let me do some kind of work in the vineyards. I needed something to keep me busy. But he refused, telling me that Dennis and his wife didn't want me around there.

"That was a lie. Dennis had asked him to bring me down to work at harvest time, and there were quite a few times that Dennis wanted to come up and visit, but Carson told him that I didn't want to see any of them. But one afternoon, Dennis did come to visit me, and that was the day that my life changed.

"I was hanging up clothes behind the house when I heard a whistle coming from the front. I was very surprised to see that it was Dennis. He was standing on the porch, holding a bouquet of wild flowers.

"He hopped down off the porch and handed the flowers to me, saying that he was hoping I would be home. Of course, he knew that it was a good bet that I would be home. Everybody knew that I didn't go off the hill very often.

"It was hot that day, and I had on a flimsy old dress that was much too tight. I never had company, so I wasn't worried about anyone seeing me like that. From the way Dennis was eyeing me, he was seeing more of me than I cared for him to see.

"Dennis wanted to know if a guy could get something to drink, 'Water would be fine if you have nothing else,' he said. He was smiling that smile that I loved, the one that was like Carson's. The one I wasn't seeing on Carson's face anymore. That smile got to me and I invited him in."

"I walked up the steps, and Dennis followed. I felt his eyes on my backside and wished that I had dressed differently that morning.

"When we got inside, I poured us a drink from the molasses bottle. I thought he deserved it. After all, he did come all the way up just to see me and brought flowers to boot.

"At first we talked about what was going on at the vineyards, but several minutes and drinks later, the conversation turned personal, and that is when Dennis told me how Carson was spending his time and with whom. I couldn't believe it. I guess that I really didn't let myself consider that Carson could do that to me. We had been together since I was fourteen and he was seventeen. But, what really surprised me was who he was hanging around with.

"I need another drink before I tell you about that. Ephriam, you do the honors." She pushed her glass toward him.

Ephriam filled her glass half way full, and started to fill Harrison's, but Harrison put his hand over his glass. Ephriam didn't take any; he was beginning to feel a little sick. Peggy then continued with her story.

"When I found out his new best friend was prissy Martha Ann, Dennis's wife, I tell you, I couldn't help but laugh. It just struck me funny; they were such an unlikely pair.

"I know for sure that Carson had never done something like that before. I really think he did it to get back at Dennis for taking away the ownership he had in the vineyards. I know that really got to Carson. For the first time in his life he had felt like he was somebody, then to have all that taken away — that really brought him down."

"I could sure see why," Ephriam said, shaking his head. "What happened after Dennis told you about Carson and Martha Ann?"

"What happened? We got drunk, that's what happened. We emptied a couple of molasses bottles, and comforted each other for a while.

"That night when Carson came in, I told him I knew he was having an affair, but I didn't tell him about Dennis' visit. He denied it and told me I was crazy. I hinted around that I knew it was Martha Ann, and he laughed about that. I told him I could understand how something like that could happen, and that I would forgive him. But he wouldn't come clean, so I decided to let it go.

"I have to confess that one of the reasons that I let it go was that I was hoping Dennis would come back to see me again, and three days later he did. After that, he would come up every few days, and I lived for his visits. I was glad that Carson was staying away from home, and I didn't care one bit who he was spending time with.

"Then one day, all hell broke loose. Carson came home and caught Dennis and me together. He went into a rage, picked Dennis up and literally threw him off the porch. Dennis took off like a scared rabbit, with no concern for what might happen to me.

"Carson came at me. He threw me on the rug, pinned me down and glared at me for what seemed like hours. It was horrible. All that night, Carson would sit and drink from one of them molasses bottles, glare at me for a while, then pick me up and throw me to the rug again. It was like he had gone mad. I was hoping he would pass out so I could escape, but he never even closed his eyes.

"By the next day, I was pretty beat up. My body was covered with bruises, and I had a gash over my right eye where he had thrown a boot at me. All that time, I thought about how it was going to end. I knew I couldn't take much more. Carson kept a loaded shotgun behind the wood box. I thought if I could threaten him with it, he would let me go. Finally, late into the second night, he nodded off. I quietly got the gun, and as soon as I had it in my hands, he woke up and asked me what the hell I was doing. I told him that if he didn't let me go, I was going to kill him. He laughed and said, 'You can't even squash a spider.' He laughed harder and started to get up.

"I was so angry. After the hell he had just put me through, he was mocking me. I heard a blast and watched as Carson grabbed his chest. Blood poured from it, and he looked up at me, and said, 'Peg…' then fell back to the floor.

"I couldn't move. I didn't remember squeezing the trigger, but Carson had a hole in his chest, and I was the one holding the gun. I was in shock, and I stood looking at him for a minute or two with the gun still pointed at him. When I came to my senses, I threw the gun down. I thought about hiding his body, and then just telling everyone that he ran off. But, after an hour of sitting and looking at the body, I thought better of it, and took off running to Dennis's house.

"I was glad Dennis was the one that answered the door. A look of disbelief came over him when he got sight of me. He grabbed me by the arm and dragged me around to the side of the house. 'Jesus Christ,' he said, what happened to you?' I told him never mind what happened to me; I was in worse trouble than having a few cuts and bruises. I told him I had shot and killed Carson.

"He said that I had to go to the police and confess, but that I wasn't to tell them about how Carson found us that day, and I wasn't to say anything at all about him coming up to my house. He said to tell them that I accused Carson of having an affair, which sent him into a rage, and that he beat me and threatened to kill me, so I shot him in self-defense.

"I promised Dennis that I would do that, but only if he would still come up and see me. He promised he would, and then he got his foreman to drive me to the police station. After seeing the condition I was in, the police believed my story."

"Does Dennis still come to see you?" Harrison asked.

"God, no, that only lasted for about two months. He began to think he owned me, and started being real mean. He said he could take this property away from me anytime he wanted. But I wasn't worried about that because after Carson's death, Martha Ann came to see me and brought some papers deeding the property to me. She said she was doing it for my protection, that women usually got taken advantage of. Isn't that something, old Martha Ann looking out for my interests? Wonders never cease. Of course, she never knew about Dennis and me."

Ephriam stood up, stretched and said, "I can see why you had to shoot Carson. You were afraid that he might kill you. It really was self defense."

"I shot him in anger, not because I thought he would kill me. When he mocked me, that was it, I wanted him dead for that reason alone. And maybe I wanted him dead so Dennis and I could continue seeing each other. I feel guilty that I wanted Carson dead for that reason, and that's why I started wearing these old clothes of his, as a reminder of what I did to him."

"Well, I still think that you had a right to kill him; he deserved to be killed," Ephriam said. "I need to use the little house out back, then we've got to get going." He walked out the door.

Ephriam searched the area around the house to see if he could spot a still. Not finding anything, he went back to the house. He opened the door, and there was no one in the room, but he could hear sounds from the back room. The dog got up and growled. Ephriam quickly shut the door, and then sat on the porch steps to wait for Harrison.

After a few minutes, Harrison came out carrying a grocery sack.

"Did you find the still?" Harrison asked.

"No, but I didn't go too far away to have a look."

"I tried to stay inside with her long enough to give you a chance to have a look around."

Harrison cleared his throat and motioned to the bag he was holding. "She said when we need more to come back and visit her."

Ephriam looked inside the bag and was happy to see two molasses bottles. He grinned. "Not a bad day's work, huh?"

Ephriam and Harrison didn't last long as agents. They weren't good at confiscating the illegal booze, and often ended up getting drunk with the bootleggers. As for Peggy, Harrison did go to see her and each time, just as she had promised, she gave him two bottles of molasses to take home. But she never revealed where she got her liquor, and one day, after Harrison insisted she tell him, she got her shotgun and ran him off. He never went back.

The Barkers continued to hunt in the winter and follow the fruit harvests in the spring. Apricots were harvested in March for about six weeks, then came almonds in early August, and after almonds would come hops.

In those days, they did everything by hand, so there was enough work for anyone who needed it. In the almond orchard, a horse would pull a long sled with canvas tarps attached. With a man at each corner, they would pull the tarps out underneath each side of the tree, then hit the limbs with rubber mallets to knock the almonds off. After doing that, they rolled the almonds into the sled, and after the sled was full, the men shoveled the nuts into sacks to take them to the huller.

The best place to work was at a hop yard, and the one the Barker family went to was the Horse Ranch, near the Russian River in Ukiah.

The Horse Ranch planted tomatoes, corn and several kinds of melons for their workers, and it wasn't bad in the camps; for one thing, there was enough food for everyone, and the kids had a great time at the river. Well, most of the time anyway, but once in a while it would be get a little dangerous, like the time Earl was knocked into the river.

It was on one of those very warm days, that Bud and Earl, along with two of their cousins, decided to cross the river where a log was used as a footbridge. The older boys decided to go across the log, and Earl being the youngest, was the tail. The older boys didn't want him to follow them, and about half way to the other side, the guy in front of Earl turned around and pushed him off. The water was deep, and it's a good thing that dog paddling is an instinct, because none of those guys were about to go into the river to save him. But he was able to make it to shore safely, and ran all the way back to the camp, cussing every step of the way.

When the family was living near Oakdale, California in 1927, they had a windmill on their property. When the mill was running, the rod would move slowly up and down, and the kids liked watching it. One day, Bud and Earl were standing there watching it go, when Teddy, who was just a toddler, waddled up, stuck his finger through the hole where the bolt had been, and off went the finger. Bud and Earl ran him home as fast as they could, and Ephriam rushed him to the doctor.

It was here that **Campbell Heiskel** was born on the fifth day of November.

In 1928, the family moved to Elk Grove and on November 14, **Benjamin Harrison** was born. They lived near town this time, and near a PG&E plant that would become the cause of a lot of worry to Johnny.

Wanted Dead or Alive by the PG&E

That summer, six-year-old Johnny was out playing when he became hungry and went inside. He found his mother in the kitchen and tugged at her skirt.

"Mama, I gotta eat or I'm gonna die. Could I get a biscuit?"

Mary laughed. "I guess I'd better hurry with supper then. I need to see about the baby first, but that won't take long. I think you can hold off for a while."

She left the room to go care for the baby, and Johnny thought she must not have understood how really hungry he was, so he looked for a biscuit, but there were none. He found potatoes on the table with a paring knife lying beside them. Not wanting to expire from hunger, he took one of the potatoes and the knife, along with a frying pan and a match, and went out to the back of the house to cook it up.

There was a barley field behind the house, and he thought that it would be the best place to do his cooking. The barley would make a good fire, and no one would see him back there.

He peeled the potato and cut it up as best he could, put it in the pan, and then went out into the middle of the field. He set the pan aside, then took the match and lit the barley. The barley exploded in flames, and Johnny panicked. He had to get the evidence out of there and hide it so no one could find out what he had done. He grabbed the pan and knife, raced to the house, and flung them underneath it.

Meanwhile, the flames were spreading fast. He ran around to the front of the house just as his mother and older brother Bud, who had seen the flames, came out the back door.

There was a PG&E power station close by, and by that time, the flames had spread to it.

The fire department came and extinguished the flames and luckily the house and garage were not damaged, but the PG&E plant was.

Johnny was afraid someone would question him, so he stayed as far away as he could, but close enough to hear someone say that the fire must have started at the power plant. Man, was he glad to hear that. Maybe he didn't have to worry about being found out after all.

However, he soon found out different, because Bud came over to him, "Johnny, I know you're the one that set that fire."

Before he had a chance to protest, Bud continued, "But you can't tell anybody this. It has to be our secret."

That was a great relief to Johnny, but something wasn't right. "Why would you want to keep it a secret?"

"What you did is a crime, and if PG&E finds out that you were the one that started that fire, they would make you pay for the plant."

"That wouldn't be so bad, because I would probably be the only kid in school that owned a power plant."

"You idiot, it would take the rest of your life to pay for it, and you would never own it."

"But I can't go to work, I haven't even started first grade yet," Johnny said.

"Even worse, you would be a wanted man, and they could hang your picture in the post office, right alongside of Al Capone's, and that would mean you could be shot on sight," Bud said.

"Okay, I'll keep the secret, but you better keep it, too. You know I'll make you mad, and then you'll probably tell on me."

"You'll just have to take that chance. Maybe you could stop doing dumb things that make me mad."

One day, Johnny was outside and saw a PG&E truck coming to the house. He hid real fast and waited until he heard the truck leave, then came out.

He didn't dare question why the truck was there—he was afraid to. He figured that Bud must have told on him. He knew that he would have to keep a lookout for the truck from then on, because it would probably be coming back again.

Sure enough, it did come back again, but luckily, Johnny was able to escape capture again. This went on for two or three more times and kept Johnny constantly worried.

One day while out rolling his hoop around, Johnny saw a big PG&E truck coming up the street with a lot of men riding in the back. They were really bringing out the big guns. He threw his hoop out in the field and made a dash to the culvert. He got far enough inside so no one could see him if they happened to look in. The truck stopped, and he heard some voices. He kept hearing the voices, but couldn't make out what they were saying. He waited quietly, hoping they would leave, but they didn't.

He whispered to himself, "Those scurby dogs ain't gonna leave until they get me. It's so hot in here, I can't last much longer."

Another vehicle came and stopped, and that disheartened him, because he couldn't stay in that pipe much longer. There were more voices. An unfamiliar one asked about the hoop and how long Johnny had been missing.

There were several loud calls of "Johnny!" He recognized that it was his mother and Bud calling.

He was getting madder by the minute. How could Bud do this to him? Even his own mother! He was a rotten kid some times, but a mother was obligated by God to protect her kids.

"I think I'll go fishing," Johnny heard Bud say.

Even though Bud had to be the stool pigeon that ratted on him, Johnny wasn't about to miss a chance to go fishing. Johnny decided he would just pop out when Bud got close.

So when he thought Bud's footsteps were at the right place, he scurried out of the pipe, right into the waiting hands of his rat brother, who dragged him back to where the others were gathered around a police car. There weren't any PG&E workers in the group; they were at the nearby plant.

Johnny's mother was happy to see him, but he was skeptical, because she was going to give him up to the police or maybe the PG&E. Heck, it didn't matter which one, he was doomed either way. She grabbed him and hugged him real tight, and he figured that it was because it was going to be his last hug from her, so she wanted to make it a good one.

Johnny waited for the police officer to get out his handcuffs, and when the officer came over to him, he didn't know whether to make a break for it or go willingly. He decided that his brother could out run him, so it wouldn't do any good to try that.

The police officer bent down, put his hand on Johnny's shoulders, and said, "I'm sure glad that you're all right."

But Johnny didn't trust him. He squinted his eyes to look real mean. *Like heck you are,* he thought, *you're just trying to soften me up before slapping the cuffs on me.*

"You sure gave your mother a scare," the officer said.

Johnny felt bad about that, but he wondered if she was feeling bad about calling the cops on him. Then something weird happened: his mother thanked the police officer, and the officer left. Maybe things weren't as he thought. But the PG&E crew was still at the plant, so he couldn't relax just yet.

After all the commotion died down, Johnny sidled up to Bud. "Hey, Bud, are you still gonna go fishing?"

Bud snickered, "I said I was going fishing because I knew that would bring you out of the pipe."

"You rotten scurby dog! I ain't never gonna trust you again."

Johnny stomped off and went inside.

Mary and Bud followed.

"Johnny, why were you hiding, and why didn't you come out when you heard us calling?" Mary asked him.

Johnny didn't say a word, just shrugged his shoulders.

Finally, Bud blurted out, "Johnny started that fire in the field, and he thought PG&E was after him for destroying their property."

Johnny glared at Bud. "You said you wouldn't tell! I knew I couldn't trust a liar like you!"

"Bud, have you known all along that Johnny started that fire?"

Bud replied sheepishly, "Yeah, Mama, I did."

"Why in the world didn't you tell us?"

Bud shrugged. "I thought that if anyone found out, Papa would have to pay for the damage."

Mary shook her head. "You should have told, Bud."

She put her hands on Johnny's shoulder and continued, "As for you, young man, you know very well you are never to touch matches. If you ever do something like this again, I'll take the shillelagh to you."

Fairzina & Campbell H. Barker

The family lived in Elk Grove until the spring of 1930, then the family traveled to Salinas, where Ephriam went to work on a ranch. There, the kids had some guinea pigs, and there were lots of apples to eat and make sauce and pies with. **Darlene Virginia** was born there on

August 30 of that year.

In January of 1931, while still living in Salinas, Ephriam got word that his father had died His father and mother hadn't moved to Salinas with him. They and Harrison had stayed in the Sacramento Valley. They would all miss the gentle, good-natured man. He died from an infection caused by getting his thumb stuck by a thorn, which caused blood poisoning to spread throughout his body.

Bud was given his grandpa's Durant touring car, which he had loved driving his grandpa around in. He especially liked that it had no top, and he felt like a million when he was in that car.

In the summer of 1931, Ephriam moved the family to a little town called Williams, and Fairzina and Harrison moved down the lane a ways from them. It was here that **Paul** was born on December 17.

A man they called the Dutchman loaned Ephriam a cow, and Mary had a few chickens for eggs and meat.

The kids would sometimes name the chickens, and it was hard for them when their pets had to be killed for food.

Black Cherry

Nine-year-old Johnny especially loved one chicken — she had shiny black feathers and he named her Black Cherry. One day, after he put her into the pen with the other chickens, she escaped. She was smaller than the others and could squeeze under the fence. He tried fixing the fence, but she continued to get out. His father told him that the chicken was a nuisance, and one of these times she wasn't going to be coming back.

The way he said it made Johnny think that his father was threatening to wring Black Cherry's neck, so he made a small pen just for her next to the big one.

She stayed in the pen for a couple of weeks, but one morning Johnny found her missing. He looked all over the place for her but didn't find her. He kept checking the pen, thinking she would come back, but when she hadn't come back by late afternoon, he knew something was wrong. She had never stayed gone that long before.

His father sometimes butchered chickens late at night to have for dinner the next day, so the thought that he may have killed Black Cherry kept popping into Johnny's head. He finally had to go into the house to question his mother on what they were having for dinner.

"Beans and cornbread," she said to Johnny's great relief. So he went back to trying to find the wayward chicken. He was walking on the road past the neighbor's house and saw that a cardboard box was stuck up in a big oak tree in the neighbor's yard. He thought it was a weird place to put a box, but the people who lived there were kind of strange, especially their ten-year-old girl, Alma.

She was a goofy girl. She would tell Johnny that she hated him all the time, but when she would come over to play with his sister Edith, Alma would end up following him around.

Curious about that box, he looked around and it didn't look like anyone was home, so he went over the fence and up the tree. He looked inside the box, and his blood ran cold. There was Black Cherry, lying in the box, not moving. He grabbed her up and went running home into the kitchen where his mother was.

"Mama, look at Cherry! She's dead!" he said and laid her gently on the table. His mother picked the chicken up and felt the little body.

"She still has a heartbeat. Get me the eyedropper from the cabinet in the bathroom. Hurry, then get me a glass of water," his mother said, rubbing Cherry's scrawny breast.

She would alternate between dropping water into Black Cherry's beak and rubbing her breast. She did this for about three minutes until there was a weak squawk, then a little louder one. Finally, Black Cherry flapped her wings, squawked like heck, and flew out of his mother's hands.

Johnny was relieved that his chicken was all right, but he was still angry with Alma. "Mama, Alma tried to kill my chicken by putting her in a box, and we gotta tell the police that we have a murderer living next door."

"Well, if she wanted Black Cherry to die, she didn't accomplish that. But I am going to talk to her folks about it. That was a cruel thing to do to someone's pet."

His mother talked to Alma's parents, and they said that Alma couldn't have done it, that she was afraid to climb trees. Johnny and the other kids knew better than that because they had seen her climb almost to the top of the tree at their house.

Then she had the nerve to come back over to play with Edith, and when she did, Johnny laid in to her big time. "You're a damned murderess, and someday you're gonna kill a person and then you'll fry, just like a piece of bacon, in the electric chair. And I'm gonna be there to watch the smoke coming out of your ears, and I'm gonna laugh my head off at you, the way you laughed when I told you Cherry had almost died."

"I did take your stupid ol' chicken, and I wanted it to die, because I hate you. All you care about is that ugly thing."

Alma wasn't allowed at the Barkers' place after that. Whenever Johnny thought about her, he wondered if she really did end up a murderess.

A Stork in a Storm

In the fall of 1932, the family was living near College City on the Wolfrum Ranch. The house was small but the barn was very big, and there was a tank house and a windmill. Everyone liked it there. The school was a mile away so that made two miles that the kids would walk every school day.

On January 25, 1933, they were having a late supper, and it was storming outside. The rain poured down so hard it sounded like a giant was stomping around on the tin roof.

They had just begun to eat when Mary called out, "Oh, no, my water just broke." She eased herself up from her chair and the back of her skirt was wet.

"Why didn't you say you were having labor pains?" Ephriam asked as he went to her.

"They've been just little ones, like the kind you get with false labor. I've had them off and on for a few days." She moaned as Ephriam took her arm.

"We better get you to the hospital." Bud, go out and start the truck."

Mary doubled over. "Ephriam, I don't think I can make it to the hospital."

Bud came back into the house. "I can't get that blasted truck started."

Ephriam yelled, "Earl, you and Johnny go get Mrs. Nash, and hurry!"

Mrs. Nash was a widow who lived about a half mile away. Johnny and Earl put on their coats and took off running as fast as they could. The rain was coming down so hard that they could barely see anything in front of them.

"Johnny, slow down!" Earl yelled.

Johnny, who was scared to death of storms, just kept running at breakneck speed, until he slipped in a mud hole and became completely covered in slime from head to toe.

Earl tried to help him up, but he just pulled Earl down with him.

"I'm going back home," Johnny sputtered, spitting mud from his mouth.

"No you're not! We've got to get Mrs. Nash to help Mama. Now come on." Earl grabbed Johnny's arm and pulled him up. He continued running, pulling Johnny along.

When they got to the Nash house, they banged on her door, but no one came. They continued to bang until finally Mrs. Nash opened the door.

"What are you boys doing out in this storm? Get in here."

After they were inside, Earl, still out of breath, said, "You gotta come to our house, Mrs. Nash. Mama's having the baby right now."

"Why didn't she go to the hospital?"

"Papa's truck wouldn't start," Johnny said.

"Well, there's no way I can walk that far in this storm. I'm not feeling all that good," Mrs. Nash said.

"Oh shit!" Johnny said.

"Young man, you watch your tongue!" Mrs. Nash said.

"Sorry, Ma'am, but we've come all this way in this lightning storm for nothing."

"I'm sure your pa can help her, and Edith is old enough to help some."

"Come on, Johnny. We'd better hurry back," Earl said.

When Johnny and **Earl** got back home, their mother was in the bedroom crying out in pain. Paul and Darlene had climbed under the table and were huddled together. The other kids sat at the table, being very quiet.

Mary let out one long, loud grunt, and then it was quiet. All of the kids looked at one another, and Benny, who had just turned four, with his lip trembling asked, "Did Mama die?" Before anyone could answer, there came a small cry from the bedroom.

Ephriam opened the door. "Edith, get the teakettle off the stove, and bring it with the wash pan."

Edith took the water in and came out a few minutes later. "You guys can go in, but don't run, and be quiet."

Benny was having nothing to do with it all. "I'm not gonna go in to see that bad baby. It hurt Mama. I don't like it."

The other kids went in, and Mary was holding Gloria. She took the blanket off so they could get a good look at her.

"She looks like an old woman," five-year-old Cam said, making a face. "Why was she born so old?"

Everyone laughed at that.

Benny came slowly into the room, and not looking at the baby, stuck his lip out and made a dive towards his mother. She pulled him up beside her.

"Benny, how do you like your new little sister? Do you want to hold her?" Mama held the baby out to him, but he slid off the bed and ran out of the room. He then came back and stuck his head inside the door; he was smiling so everything was okay with him.

The family was still in College City in 1934 when on June 26, **Jackie** and **Jimmie,** the only set of twins Mary and Ephriam had, were born in the Colusa County Hospital.

UPPER LAKE NEWS ITEMS. | Agricultu
News Iten

Tuesday, 26 June 1934, Colusa Sun-Herald
College City Woman, 36, Mother of 14, Gives Birth to Twins (head lines on front page)
Mary Barker
Couple Now Have 11 boys And 3 Girls
Metzger, Senate Candidate Gives Champion Mother Gifts For Babies
The Dionne family set the world agog with quintuplets a month ago but they are far from the record of Mr. and Mrs. Ephriam B. Barker, who today held the distinction of having Colusa county's largest family, or nearly so if this claim is disputed.
Twin sons, the 15th and 16th children, were born at a hospital here today to Mrs. Mary Barker, wife of a College City farmer, who is only 36 years old. Fourteen of the children, 11 boys and 3 girls, are living, including the twins, a boy and a girl dying in infancy. Both mother and twins are doing nicely. So impressed was D. J. (Jack) Metzger, mayor of Red Bluff and candidate for state senator, that he called at the hospital while here today and presented the champion mother with a gift for each of the new babies.
Husky Babies
Interviewed at the hospital today by a Sun-Herald reporter, Mrs. Barker said she had about "run out of names" and was at a loss to know what to name the twins. The twins are husky babies. The first one, weighing 6 1/2 pounds, was born at 12:50 a. m. today and the other, 7 3/4 pounds, 15 minutes later. Asked how she manager such a large family, Mrs. Barker replied: "Well, I think I have an easier time managing a large family than some people do with small ones." The Barkers live on the old Tolson place in College City.
Their first boy, who died, would have been 20 years old this month, and the girl who died at the age of 3 years, would have been 16, Mrs. Barker said.

Jackie & Shep—Jimmie & Snowball

Indian Valley

In August of 1924, Ephriam decided to locate his homestead in Indian Valley in the mountains of Lake County, California, about forty-miles from Lakeport, the county seat.

He chose a flat area near the old Hough (pronounced Huff) Springs Resort that had a creek running through it. There was a tollhouse that was used in the 1800s for the Epperson toll road that ran through the property. The road at that time was called Bartlett Springs Road.

For about 5,000 years, Indians inhabited the area, and it was around 1860 that Lake County was formed. Some of the first settling in this area was a Mr. Sawtelle, Greene Bartlett, George Allen and Frank Kowalski. Mr. Sawtelle never proved up his homestead, but Frank Kowalski did and eventually ended up owning quite a bit of the valley.

Frank Kowalski owned much of the southern end of the valley in the 1880s and '90s. In 1911, he married Rosalie Vergnes, a widow with five children, who had bought property in the northern part of the valley. With their combined acreage, they owned a large portion of the valley. They raised cattle and grew hay and grain.

Lake County had many mineral springs and that led to the opening of many resorts. The naturally hot mineral baths were thought to be a beneficial treatment for almost all diseases, and a cure for many. One such hot springs resort was Bartlett Springs, which Greene Bartlett started with the building of a few crude cabins in 1870; in 1873 he built a two-story hotel and more cabins. Bartlett sold to the McMahon family, who expanded it to include five hotels, several cottages and became incorporated. It was listed as a first class resort in 1892. It remained open until 1934.

In 1985, Vittel Mineral Water Company of France started bottling

Bartlett Spring's water at a plant they had opened up in Nice, California. They were supposedly going to restore the resort. Not sure if that happened.

Hot spring resorts were very popular in those early days and they had many famous visitors. In 1892, Gentleman Jim Corbett trained at Bartlett Springs for his bout, which he won, with John L. Sullivan, who was training at a nearby resort, Harbin Springs. Also, Queen Marie from Rumania stayed at Bartlett Springs.

On the south side of the north fork of Cache Creek, Sylvanus Hough and his son Orlando, discovered a flow of mineral water, and around 1880, Orlando and his mother started the Hough Springs Resort.

Earlier, a family by the name of Anderson started a resort nearby, but it hadn't been successful, so Sylvanus Hough purchased their hotel, dismantled it, and used the lumber to build a two-story hotel at Hough Springs.

BARKERSVILLE BRIEFS

Marcel McComb Meets With Gun Accident

Marcel McCombs, who has spent this last winter at Hough Springs, accidentally shot himself in the leg while hunting here last week. He walked two miles on his injured leg to get medical aid and later was taken to a hospital in Ukiah where X-rays showed a fractured bone. Mr. McCombs expects to return to his home in Upper Lake as soon as the cast is put on his leg.

Mr. and Mrs. Earl DeSoto and son of Berkeley spent the weekend at their cabin at Bartlett Springs.

Mr. and Mrs. Henry Elphick of Sebastopol spent several days visiting with Dr. J. P. Miller.

Mr. and Mrs. Clarence Keister of Stockton are house guests at Dr. Miller's home here this week.

Hough Springs became a successful resort with a hotel, hot mineral baths, cottages, a store, gas station, post office, a Sunday school and a dancehall.

Between the time it opened and closed for good, it was bought and sold a few times, finally closing in 1920, and then was sold to George Abel in 1921.

Around 1871, about three miles from Hough Springs, on a tributary of the north fork of Cache Creek, a man named George Allen discovered there were mineral springs there and thought it would be a good place to have a resort. He and his brother Vale started the Allen Springs resort.

Around 1878, they built a hotel along side the toll road that ran from Bear Valley to Bartlett Springs, and by 1881, the resort not only had hot mineral and steam baths, there was also a barbershop, billiard room, dancehall, post office and a telegraph station. They also bottled the mineral water there.

In the early part of the 1900s, there was some flooding of the creeks that washed out several of the buildings and the resort closed for a while, reopening in 1910.

The popularity of mineral water died down, and with the coming of cars and better roads, lengthy vacations were not as prevalent. And with electricity coming to the towns and the opening of resorts around the lakes, the isolated resorts lost a lot of their clientele. Consequently, by the early 1930s most were no longer operating.

There were some interesting events, including murders, that happened up in those mountains during those early days and the following stories are based on them.

Kurdy Glade Murder

Kurdy Glade was named for a man from Arizona who had come to dig for gold in the area in the 1870s. He brought with him two men: brothers Tudd and Jake. Tudd, who was the elder of the two, had managed to save some money and had a team of horses and a wagon.

One morning the three men got up early and made plans to do some digging at the shaft they had started. Jake started out very early, and Tudd, who had twisted his ankle a couple of days earlier, was still in quite a bit of pain, so he was to ride one of the horses out a little later. Kurdy told them that he was going to do a little fishing before going to the shaft, so they could have some fish for supper.

About three hours later, just as Tudd was getting ready to leave camp, Kurdy came back and told him that his brother wasn't at the mine. He told him that after fishing for about thirty minutes, and not catching any fish, he went to the shaft, and when he got there, Jake was nowhere around. He said he worked for a couple of hours, and when Jake never showed up, he thought he'd better go back to camp and see if he was there.

Tudd was suspicious. This wasn't something his brother would do. Taking his gun, he went with Kurdy to look for Jake, but kept on the alert, always staying at least three feet behind Kurdy.

They went to the shaft, and as soon as they got near the pit, Jake's body could be seen lying in the middle of it. Tudd went to see what had happened; still making sure Kurdy was in front of him. When they reached Jake, who was lying face down, Tudd bent down, and when he did, Kurdy started to lift his rifle up. But Tudd had expected Kurdy to try something, and he lunged at Kurdy's legs and knocked him to the ground. He wrestled the gun from him, tied him up, and after seeing that there wasn't anything he could do for Jake, whose head was split open by a pickaxe, he took Kurdy to the marshal's office in Lakeport.

There was no problem in convicting Kurdy of murder, and shortly after being sent to prison, another inmate killed him.

Kurdy's plan was to take Tudd to the mine and pretend that he had not seen Jake there that morning so Tudd would think someone else killed Jake. People figured that Kurdy planned to kill Tudd later, make it look like an accident, and then with the two brothers out of the way, he would have the mine all to himself. But he must have sensed that Tudd was suspicious of him and decided that he better not wait to get rid of him.

Jake's ghost has been seen sitting where the entrance to the shaft used to be, with his head in his hands. And blood-curdling screams have been heard, but that just might have been a panther; they have a scream like someone who is being murdered.

Epperson Tollhouse Murder

One mile upstream from Indian Valley, on the north fork of Cache Creek, is a flat area that once had a tollgate for the Epperson Toll Road. The road went from Bartlett Springs down to the stage station and beyond to Complexion Canyon. This area would later become known as Barkersville.

Around 1893, a murder happened in this area. The killer was Bill Williams, the tollgate keeper for the Epperson Toll Road, and the victim was Jerry Sullivan, who had been living at Anderson Springs Resort since the previous owner vacated it.

Williams and Sullivan had a falling out over some lies that Sullivan supposedly told about Williams. Williams sent word to Sullivan that he wanted to talk with him, and that he should come over to the tollhouse.

Sullivan went to the tollhouse, and when Williams came to the door, he had a gun in his hand. Sullivan turned and ran, but Williams shot him in the back and killed him.

After the shooting, Williams tried to make it look as though Sullivan had fired at him first. He took Sullivan's gun out of its holster and shot himself in the thigh, just grazing it, and then put the gun down by Sullivan's side.

Williams tried to convince a jury it was self-defense. He said that on that day, he was inside the tollhouse when he heard Sullivan call his name. He said that by the sound of Sullivan's voice, he knew that he was angry, so he took his gun when he opened the door to protect himself in case there was any trouble. He said that as soon as he opened the door, Sullivan shot at him, wounding his leg, and when he fired back, Sullivan had turned and that's why he was shot in the back. He took his trousers with the bullet hole in the leg to court to try and prove his story, but the prosecutor showed that the powder burns on them proved his wound was self-inflicted. Williams went to prison where he died after a few years.

Sullivan was buried at Anderson Springs Resort, where the terrace of the old hotel had been. Some say his spirit still roams the area where the old tollhouse once stood.

A Murder & a Haunted House

Down by the Old Road House, there was a ramshackle cabin that used to be a stage stop, and the old man that herded sheep around there told everyone that if they were going past that place not to stop and fool around because it was haunted. He said that a stage driver was shot and killed while being robbed somewhere on Leesville grade, and a young girl that was riding with him was wounded.

The stagecoach made it to the cabin, and the girl managed to get off and crawl to the porch.

She pulled herself up to the window, put her hand on it, and then fell dead. There was a trail of blood across the porch and a bloody handprint on the windowpane.

The incident really did happen. People passing by there at night report hearing voices in the cabin and hearing a girl crying. The old sheepherder said that at night you could see the girl's bloody handprint on the windowpane.

Spanish Ridge Murder

A stream runs into Cache Creek, which is also called Spanish Creek. In the late 1800s, a Spaniard who was living several miles up the creek ran cattle for a living. He supposedly sold his stock for gold coins. There were rumors that he buried these coins somewhere in those mountains, and after one of his runs, a couple of drifters followed him back to his cabin and waited for him to go inside.

They followed him in and insisted that he give them all his proceeds from his sale that day. He handed over one gold coin and a receipt from the cattle buyers, which stated that he was paid by a bank note. After taking the coin, they tried to make him tell where he had his other gold coins buried, but he insisted that he had no other coins, and the methods they rendered in trying to make him talk caused him to lose consciousness.

The men tore the little cabin apart but didn't find anything, so they went out and searched around the place. They left no leaf or rock unturned and dug where it looked like the earth had been upturned. They did this for a couple of hours, then went back inside to see if the Spaniard was ready to talk, but they found that he had died, so they hightailed it out of those mountains as fast as their old nags would take them.

These men, who were obviously not too swift, arrived back in town a couple of days later, and the first place they headed was to the saloon. One of them slapped the stolen coin on the bar, and the barkeep, not getting many gold coins from his customers, inquired of them how they came to have it. They told him that they did some work for a cattle runner who paid them with the coin.

They told the same story to other patrons and many of them, and the barkeep, became suspicious. But there wasn't anything to prove that their story wasn't true, and soon the drifters drank up and left town.

About one week after that, a trapper found the Spaniard. When the people who witnessed the gold coin incident at the bar heard about the death, they knew their suspicions were correct. But by then the drifters had left town and were probably never caught for that crime.

The gold coins were never found and it has been reported that the ghost of the Spaniard can be seen digging for his coins near the place where he lived.

Ann Herds Turkeys to Market

In the early 1920s, Ann Newton, a widow living alone on Spanish Ridge, made her living raising turkeys. In the fall, she would take them to the market in Williams, a town about thirty-five miles away. She herded them all the way by horseback, with her two hound dogs keeping the turkeys in line.

She would start early in the morning, making sure the horse, turkeys and dogs were well fed and watered. She took her bedroll, a few biscuits, and enough venison jerky for herself and the dogs.

The first place she stopped on her journey was Hough Springs, to water the animals and to rest a spell. She didn't linger long and was soon herding her gobblers down the road again.

She had to get to a certain spot before nightfall; it had a tree that was good for the turkeys to roost in, and a small tree nearby, under which she would bed down.

There were several more stopping places, as this was a long trek.

There was grass along the way for the horses, the turkeys would have no problem finding insects of all sorts, and there were springs every few miles so they would have water.

Somehow, she and the dogs managed to keep those turkeys in line and delivered them to market without too much wear and tear.

She used what money she received to stock up on provisions. She loaded up her saddlebags with flour, beans, lard, sugar, coffee, canned milk, potatoes and a side of bacon. She would purchase all the threads she would need for her embroidery and knitting, and she made sure she got plenty of tobacco for the pipe that had comforted her through all the hard times since her husband died in his sleep in 1919.

The pipe had belonged to her husband and one day, soon after his death, she had found it lying on his chair on the porch. She got the urge to light it up, and then she sat down in the chair, closed her eyes and proceeded to smoke. After a few minutes of puffing, she envisioned him smiling down on her, and she could feel his presence.

The smell brought back pleasant memories of their evenings sitting on their porch, with her doing needlework as he puffed on his pipe and told stories. The stories had been there inside him for years, just waiting to be told to the children they were supposed to have. But there were never any children, so she pretended to delight in every word of those stories, as a child would have.

Her husband, whom she called Newt, was a trapper and hunter and that was how they ended up on Spanish Ridge. He had come to the area a few times and had such success that he decided that they should move there. Of course, Ann had to follow, but she didn't mind. Newt was her everything; she would have followed him to hell if need be. They had married when she was fifteen and he was a strapping lad of eighteen.

Early in 1900, Newt met Adam Wylie while both were trapping along Spanish Creek. Adam was a bachelor; a forlorn-looking man, small of stature, but he had a big heart. He was Newt's only close friend (besides Ann).

Adam had lost an arm in a trapping accident. He'd gotten it caught in a trap while trying to set it and eventually had to have it removed because it wouldn't heal. Newt was with him at the time of the accident, and it was lucky for Adam that he was. He could never have removed the trap by himself and would have bled to death if Newt had not removed it and got him medical help.

Ann never really got over Newt's death, and if it were not for Adam being close by, she would have probably left that God forsaken place.

It has been said that the reason Adam never married was his love for Ann; that could've been just a rumor, but if was true, and she and Adam got together after Newt's death, then maybe that makes for a happy conclusion for two lonely people who had both lost their best friend. But if they did get together, it didn't last long as Adam died from heart failure in the summer of 1923 after being in poor health for a year or more.

Ann, once again filled with grief, decided to stay on at Spanish Ridge, even though some who knew her said she should leave. But she couldn't imagine leaving the place that had meant so much to her—the place that held the memories of the two men who had been her companions most of her adult years. Occasionally, she would get a visitor or would trek over to the Abel's place, but she preferred to be alone with just her dogs, horse, turkeys and pipe for company.

Barkersville

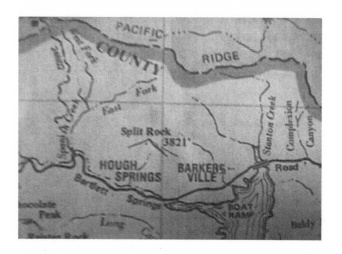

Oone early morning in August of 1934, Elden "Bud" Barker cursed as he came out the back door of his family's home.

"Blasted heat! We're gonna burn up today." He mopped sweat from his brow as he walked over to the old Yellow Cab Company truck that was to take the family to their new homestead.

"This move is going to be our last," his father had said, the first time he took the family up to see the site he had chosen for their homestead.

When the older boys—Bud, 18; Earl, 15; Johnny, 12; and Bobby, 11—got a picture of all the work that needed to be done, even the ability to fish and swim at any time, and hunt and trap with no restrictions, became of less importance.

The younger boys—Teddy, 9; Pat, 8; Cam, 7; Benny, 6 and Paul, 3—were excited about going up in the mountains where they would be

66

living near a creek, and could not wait to get there.

Mary was not pleased about moving to the mountains, she liked the wide-open spaces. She was born near the Black Hills in South Dakota, and her first memories were of the prairie.

But from the first time she had viewed the homestead site, she had tried to convince herself that this was going to be a good thing. Maybe it would be permanent, she was so tired of the moving and she knew it wasn't good for the children.

Bud hoisted himself into the cab of the truck and tried to start it, but temperamental "Old Yellow" wouldn't cooperate. Anger erupted from the tall, blue-eyed eighteen-year-old. "Damn-it-to-hell! You rotten piece of junk!"

It wasn't only the heat and the truck that peeved Bud—no, his fowl mood was mostly because he was leaving his girlfriend and going up into some God-forsaken country with only a lot of hard work to look forward to.

Bud tried to start the truck again, but it just groaned.

Bud's younger brother Johnny, yanked the passenger door open and climbed in.

"What in the hell are you doing? You've got it flooded."

Johnny was big for his twelve years. He was almost as tall as Bud and weighed a few pounds more. He wore a hat that he would cock at an angle on his brown hair, and his mischievous blue eyes often seemed to taunt, "I know something that you don't." According to Johnny, he knew almost everything about everything, and he didn't hesitate to let that fact be known.

"What do you know about it? You never started this thing before," Bud said.

Johnny handed Bud the cup of coffee he had brought out to him. "Smell that gas? Let it set for a few minutes. Then try again, and don't pump the gas pedal so much next time."

Bud was usually easy to get along with, but Johnny picked the wrong morning to give his opinion.

"I know it's flooded, but I didn't pump the damned gas pedal. There's something wrong with this piece of junk. We shouldn't be driving it any place."

"We'll make it all right, but the problem will be when it overheats going up the Leesville grade. We're gonna have to fill that drum over there with water and take it along."

Bud looked at his brother, who was always trying to be in charge of everything. "My head is about to explode and I don't need any guff from you. I'm gonna go inside to get some aspirins."

As soon as Bud got out of the truck, Johnny slid under the steering wheel, waited a couple of minutes, and then turned the key. The truck started just as Bud was coming back out of the house.

"Smart ass," Bud said. "Drive the truck around to the front so we can load up."

Loading up took longer than it normally would have because of the heat. They would stop, go under the big oak to hose off and get a drink, and then start again.

After everything was loaded, Bud took off toward Anita's house. He worried that this might be the last time he would see her for a few days. He was used to seeing her every evening, and even though he planned to visit her every weekend, that wouldn't be enough. He wondered if some other guy was going to make a move on her. He was sure that Denman Taylor would try. He was a punk that thought he was God's gift to women.

Eight-year-old Pat, who was even more tenacious than Johnny, had followed Bud and came running back a few minutes later.

He went to where Bobby, a very serious eleven-year-old, was pumping water into a bucket and said softly, "Bud and Anita are in the backseat of that old Buick that's in the back of her house."

Bobby wasn't one who needed to know what everyone else was doing. He hated that Johnny and Pat were always nosing around in everybody else's business.

"It's none of your business what Bud is doing. Go on in the house and help Mama." Bobby was disgusted with Pat.

"You're not my boss. I think Papa would like to know what those guys are doing in—"

Bobby threw water into Pat's face, and said as Pat sputtered, "If you do that, I have a few things to tell Pa about you. Go on in the house before I clobber you."

Pat decided that he better do what Bobby said, but before he did, he went to seven-year-old Cam who was playing with an anthill under the oak tree in the front yard and told him what he saw Bud doing. Cam was usually Pat's accomplice in his shenanigans.

"Let's go back there," Cam said.

Bobby overhead. "You two better not leave this yard. Go in the house, right now!"

They went with Pat mumbling under his breath, "This stupid family never wants a kid to have any fun."

Inside the empty house, Mary and Edith were feeding the twins their bottles, Paul and Gloria were both whining, and Gloria needed a diaper change. Little Darlene, although only four, offered to change Gloria.

Mary laughed. "You can sit right here beside Edith. I'll put Jackie on your lap so you can finish giving him his bottle, and I'll change Gloria."

That made Darlene even happier, and Mary had Benny sit with her. Benny, who was six, was a little man. He loved to be asked to help with anything and was so accommodating. Paul, who was a year or so younger than Darlene, came and sat with her as well. He was always by Darlene's side. She was his little mother.

Bud was in better spirits when he came back from Anita's. She promised him she would never look at another guy, especially Denman, whom she said was a real jerk. Bud wished that she wasn't so pretty, although he knew if she weren't, he wouldn't be with her.

The little ones were all very cranky by the time they were ready to leave. Everyone was irritable from the heat, and for Mary, who was no stranger to moving, this was going to be even harder, for she had the two-month-old twins to care for. And it would be hard for Edith, who was fourteen, as she would be helping with the little ones. Of course, the older boys would help to look after the younger ones.

It was late afternoon before everything and everyone was loaded into Old Yellow and the Durant. Bud, Johnny and Teddy rode in the truck's cab. Bobby, Pat, Cam and Benny were in the back, stuck amongst all the cargo. Ephriam, Mary, Jackie, Jimmie, Edith, Gloria, Paul and Darlene rode in the Durant.

Fifteen-year-old Earl decided to stay in College City with the Friel family. He didn't want to go up into the mountains.

The trip took longer than expected; along with the usual problems, like kids wanting water after the jugs were empty and having to stop so they could relieve themselves, there were some unexpected problems. Well … maybe not all that unexpected, because when you move a lot, Murphy's Law is always along for the ride—especially on a scorching day in August, loaded down with kids and cargo, in a truck that is in questionable condition.

Going up Leesville grade, they had to stop and let the truck cool off several times. It was a good thing they had brought the big drum of water. After making it up Leesville grade, they hit Brim grade and made it to the big wide corner where the waterfall was, a good place to rest. Everyone soaked themselves and rested while the truck cooled off. When Bud tried to start the truck again, it wouldn't turn over.

"We're going to stay here tonight," Ephriam said. "Let's get the mattresses off and line them up under those pine trees."

They had learned from experience to put the mattresses and blankets at the top of the load, in case they had to stop for the night. They lay out the six mattresses, side by side, and after a supper of the bologna and bread that Mary had brought along, they collapsed on the beds, and everyone was asleep as soon as their heads touched the pillows.

Everyone that is, except Mary. Besides the twins, noises kept her awake most of the night. Ephriam kept his gun handy though, in case animals or strange people approached them.

Around 2:30 in the morning, a car drove in and parked in front of the waterfall. Mary shook Ephriam awake. He sat up, grabbed his rifle, and waited to see what they were up to.

Two men got out of the car, and it sounded like they were relieving themselves. Afterwards, they walked over to where the mattresses were laid out and stopped. One turned on a flashlight and shined it over the brood.

"What the hell do you think you're doing?" Ephriam asked. He pointed the rifle at the man with the flashlight.

Bud, Bobby, and Johnny rose up, and Bud said, "You better get the hell out of here, or you're going to be dead in just about a minute."

"Okay, okay! We're leaving. We thought you might be some friends of ours, that's all," the one with the flashlight said. They retreated in haste back to their car.

After the car left, Mary worried even more about the area where they were going to live. She stayed awake the rest of the night. When it was daylight, she woke Ephriam and asked him to build a fire so she could make some coffee. He made a campfire, and Mary made her coffee. For breakfast, they finished off the rest of the bologna and bread. After the drum and water jugs were filled at the waterfall, they were ready to try to make it up Brim grade.

Bud got the truck started and they began the climb up the hill. But it kept overheating, and when that happened, they would have to wait until it cooled off, fill it with water, and try again. They did this all the way up to the homestead.

When they finally did arrive at the spot where they would settle, it was mid-morning. The first thing that Ephriam and the kids did was to take a swim in the creek. There was a perfect place to do that where the creek was the deepest, and there was a huge rock jutting out of the bank to jump from.

Barkersville

Mary sat on the rock with Edith, watching the kids splashing and laughing, and she felt better. Seeing her children happy and healthy was the most important thing in her life. They faced so many hardships, and any moments of happiness they had made everything easier for her to bear. She liked the area that Ephriam had chosen—the creek was wonderful, and the hill behind it would be a good place for a house.

Teddy stepped out of the creek and was getting ready to climb up to where his mother was sitting when there was a rattling, buzzing noise.

"Teddy, don't move. That's a rattler," Mary cried.

Ephriam heard what Mary said and got out of the water. He picked up a big rock and went to where Teddy stood motionless. The rattlesnake was at the base of the rock that Mary and Edith were on, about three feet from Teddy. It was coiled with its tongue lashing out and its rattles going at full force. He slammed the rock down on it. He picked up a few other rocks and threw them on it.

Visibly shaken, Mary herded all her kids back into the car and truck.

"Ephriam, you and the boys go hunt up all the rattlers you can find in this area. We're not getting out of this truck until you do."

Ephriam and the older boys searched for rattlers. They found five. Ephriam shot two with his twenty-two; Bud, Johnny, and Bobby killed the ones they found with rocks. Bud and Johnny removed the rattles, and the one that Bud killed had 12 rattles; it was a big snake.

Ephriam and the boys put up a big tent on the flats by the creek, close to the old tollhouse, and then they unloaded the truck. They put the kitchen things and Ephriam and Mary's bed in the tollhouse. Everything else went in the tent.

The next few days were spent surveying the property. Johnny ran transit, and Bud and Bobby marked the boundaries by making chips in trees. After that, they helped their father put up a cabin made out of the lumber from an old building nearby that had fallen down.

A family of homesteaders lived across the creek from where the Barker family had settled. They were the Turners: Lucien, his wife Judy, and their children, Tina and Melvin. Another homesteading family, the Saylors—Jim, his wife Lela, and their children, Alafair and Roy—lived on the flats close to the creek.

When Ephriam and his boys began to build the cabin, the Turners came over and offered to help, and their help was surely appreciated.

They helped until the cabin was raised, and on the day it was completed, there was a little celebration. It was deer season, so Ephriam and Bud went hunting early that morning, and Bud killed a four-pointer. Mary baked a huge venison roast, Mrs. Turner made a cake, and they set up a table made from the leftover wood from the house.

Jim Saylor was working out of town, but Lela and her children came to the celebration. Lela brought a couple of elderberry pies and some corn on the cob, which was roasted in a pit that Johnny dug.

Pat and Bobby over to the Abel's place at nearby Hough Springs to invite them, and they came over, bringing some apple cider.

Ephriam got out his banjo, Mr. Abel brought his fiddle, and they played good old-fashioned bluegrass all afternoon. The kids sang along.

After the get-together, Mary was feeling better about their move, but the Lake County school district wasn't.

An article appeared in the *Lake County Bee*, September 1934:

New Lake County Family Has 14 Children; School is Needed.

When Ephriam Barker and his wife Mary moved into Lake County a few weeks ago bringing with them fourteen children, of whom eight are of school age, county officials would have appreciated it if they had brought with them a school building and a private tutor.

The authorities face the legal requirement of constructing a one family edifice and hiring a special instructor, for the Barkers have settled in Indian valley, which is not part of any school district.

When the Barker family is all together on the 8 acres they are clearing for a future farm, the number, besides the parents — Jack and Jim, 3-month-old twins — Gloria, 2 — Paul 3 — Darlene 4 — Benny 6 — Cam 7 — Pat 8 — Teddy 9 — Bobby 11 — John 12 — Edith 14 — Earl 15 and Elden 16.

Under the compulsory education law — Bennie — Cam — Pat — Teddy — Bobby — John — Edith and Earl — must attend school. The same law imposes up on the county officials the responsibility of providing school facilities where there are eight or more children of school age. Mr. Barker anticipates adding a room to his new home and renting it to the county as a classroom. He expects to be chairman of a school board, of which the other member, his wife, will act as secretary. In a few years Edith may be the schoolteacher, and as fast as one child graduates, another will have come along to fill the needed number.

All what was in that article never materialized, and they ended up using a Hough Springs building as the schoolhouse. It was located down gravel road that tortured bare feet. The teacher was Mrs. Nelson, and later a Mr. Vail.

Barkersville

Schoolhouse

That same year, a Civilian Conservation Corps Camp was put up across the creek from the homestead. They put up buildings and had quite a few young men come in. The CCC was started by FDR. in order to employ the unemployed young men affected by the Great Depression. There were hundreds of camps set up throughout the United States and about three million young men served between 1933 and 1942 when it was disbanded.

The young men were paid twenty-five dollars a month — twenty was sent home to the family, and the enlistee kept five. The camp across the creek from the Barkers was in operation from 1934 to 1939.

Johnny was one of the CCC boys for a while. He joined when he was thirteen years old, under Earl's name, and was at the Spike Camp in Gualala, California. He didn't stay long though. He said that the cots were only about ten inches apart, and there was so much snoring that he couldn't sleep at all.

About a month after the Barkers moved in, and only a few days after the get-together, the Turners decided to abandon their homestead, telling Ephriam he could tear down the house and use the lumber to build a bigger place. Mr. Turner never had much help on his place, and it just wasn't being proved up like it was supposed to be.

The Barkers were sad to see the Turners leave, but they were glad to be able to build a larger house. They built the house on the side of the hill above the flats, right below the spring where they got their water. The spring had been there for years; it was the water source for the old tollhouse.

There was a bunkhouse built for the boys on the left side of the house, and an outhouse was put on the right of the house, a little farther up the hill. It was at this time that the homestead became known as Barkersville.

In the spring of 1935, Ephriam's brother Seaton moved up and established his place about a mile downstream. His family consisted of his wife, Minnie, daughters, Jeanette and Marilyn, and son, Seaton Junior.

Seaton was the star route mail carrier for a lot of years in Colusa County. He would also bring up food and freight from town for people who lived in the Indian Valley area, and give them rides to town if need be. All star route carriers did those kinds of things in those days.

Uncle Seaton's Family

There is an interesting story of how he got that job, and you can see that something like that could never happen these days, and it's a good thing that it can't.

You see, when a very pretty girl named Minnie Robinson worked as a waitress at the Senator Hotel in Sacramento, she was well liked by all the politicians that came to the hotel restaurant for lunch. And after she became romantically involved with Seaton, she convinced one of those guys to fire the mail carrier that had that route and hire Seaton to replace him.

That was not a very fair thing to do, and it upset the fired mail carrier and on his last day, he went and scattered the sacks of mail all over the mountainside.

To some outsiders, Seaton became known as "poor Barker" or "little Barker" while Ephriam was known as "rich Barker" or "big Barker". This had nothing to do with wealth, but originated from the fact that Seaton had four children, and Ephriam at that time had sixteen.

With all the work that was required to prove a homestead, people thought that the larger the family, the greater chance of succeeding and with success, the more a family would prosper. Of course, it did not always work out that way.

The Homestead

A Dream Lost

Despite all the work they had to do, the kids loved the freedom they had to roam the mountains, fish, hunt, trap and explore.

Even Bud, who hadn't been enthused about living in the mountains, was beginning to appreciate the homestead, and he was able to go see Anita almost every weekend, so things weren't too bad.

Bud was happy on that Saturday before Christmas as he and his father left for the valley to deliver firewood. In Colusa, he went into the five and dime and bought a gold chain with a dainty little cross. He had the clerk wrap it, and he got a card to go with it.

They made the deliveries in Colusa, then went to College City and delivered the rest of the wood. When Ephriam stopped for gas, Bud told him that he would walk the rest of the way to Anita's, and that he would catch a ride with someone when he wanted to go home. Bud whistled as he walked down the road to Anita's house. He was going to see his girl.

But something wasn't right when he neared her house. There wasn't the usual loud music coming from the radio that Anita kept going from morning to night.

"I hope she's not gone." He knocked on the door but there was no answer. He knocked several more times to no avail.

He hadn't been able to tell her that he would be there that day, but they had an understanding that she would stay home every Saturday, in case he got a chance to come see her.

He looked in the windows that were in the front, and it looked like there was no one home.

He walked around to the back and heard some voices. He thought that maybe someone just got home, and turned to go back to the front. But then he heard a loud giggle, and it was coming from the car that he and Anita had spent so much time in.

He quietly walked over to it, and what he saw sent his happy mood plunging. Anita was with Denman in back seat. Bud stood, transfixed.

"Bud!" Anita cried out.

Denman jerked his head around to face Bud. He quickly moved away from Anita. What the..."

"Bud, what are you doing here?" Anita asked.

Bud opened the door and pulled Denman out. He sent a right hook to Denman's jaw.

Denman fell to the ground, and Anita scrambled out of the car and ran toward the house.

As soon as Bud turned his attention toward Anita, Denman hopped up and bolted like a rat chased by a terrier.

Bud caught up with Anita at the back door of the house. "I thought you hated him!"

Anita started to cry. "Come inside so we can talk."

Bud followed her inside. She told him to sit on the couch, and then she went to the kitchen and came back with two beers.

"Bud, I want you to know that I don't really like Denman. You are the one I want to be with." She reached for him, but he pushed her away.

"You don't give a damn about me." Bud chugged the beer down, then asked for another. Anita went to the kitchen, but she brought back a bottle of whiskey instead of beer.

After Bud took a few gulps, Anita took the bottle and drank from it. They sat in silence for a couple of minutes. Anita tried putting her arms around him again, but he pushed her away.

Anita took a few more drinks from the bottle, and then broke the silence.

"I've got something to tell you. It's about something my doctor told me last year."

"Your doctor? Are you sick?"

"In a way, I am."

Bud frowned. "What the hell does that mean?"

"I'm going to explain it to you. Please try to understand."

Bud took another swig and looked at the almost empty bottle. "Explain away then."

"Bud, there is something wrong with me. I can't resist men. My doctor says it's because I never had a father figure in my life. I crave the attention of men. I can't help myself."

"That's bull. That kind of woman is just a tramp, that's all."

"Didn't you ever wonder why I was always bugging you to go out to the car, even when you didn't want to?"

"I thought that was because you loved me."

"Bud, I do love you, but like I told you, I can't help myself."

Bud was feeling the effects of the whiskey and he laid his head back He had to believe Anita. She wouldn't lie about something that sick.

Anita slowly scooted closer until she was touching Bud. He put his arm around her and pulled her close, letting her have the closeness she craved.

Bud had mixed feelings about Anita. He really did care for her, but he didn't think he could have a relationship with her anymore. He saw her a few more times after that, but in the spring of the following year, she and her mother moved away from the area.

Kids Play with Live Ammunition

In November of 1934, Ephriam and Mary, along with Edith and the younger children, left in the morning to go to Colusa to do some errands. They left twelve-year-old Johnny in charge of Bobby, Pat, Cam and Benny. This was only done because a CCC Camp was close by, and it would only take a few minutes to get help if some emergency happened. There was a doctor at the camp at all times.

It was raining when they started out that morning, and they hurried with their errands in town so they could get back home as early as possible. They especially wanted to be home before dark. They didn't want the children to be alone at night, and they knew Johnny was terribly afraid of the dark.

It was late afternoon when they left Colusa and started up the mountain. There was a pouring rain and the roads were muddy. It was a slow trip because of the weather, and it was dark when they got to the bottom of Leesville grade. They stopped there so Ephriam could chain up the Durant.

Jim Saylor was behind them, driving a '28 Model A Coupe, and he had to chain up too but was faster than Ephriam, and when he finished, he came up Ephriam's car.

He said, "You've gotta get out of the way, Buck, something bad has happened up there."

Ephriam asked, "What do you mean?"

Jim told him, "I said get out of the way; I've got to get up there. Something bad has happened up in those mountains."

After saying that, he ran back to his car and took off, barely making it around the Durant.

Before Ephriam got up the grade, a truck came down the hill there at Leesville. Ephriam pulled over to let the truck pass, but it stopped when it got beside the car. Jim Saylor and a couple of other guys were in the truck.

Jim stuck his head out the window. "Buck, they're taking Bobby to the hospital. He got shot."

Mary let out a cry and started to get out of the car, but Ephriam held her back.

"I've got to see him!" Mary said.

"He's going to be all right," Jim said. "They have to get him to the hospital fast because of the bleeding. Take Mary and the kids home, and I'll go to the hospital with Bobby. We'll come back up and let you know how he's doing. You and Mary can come down early in the morning."

As soon as they got home, Ephriam and Mary immediately took Johnny aside. Ephriam asked, "What happened here today, Johnny?"

Johnny couldn't look either of them in the eye. He felt so bad. "Just before dark, I thought I heard a panther scream. One of the boys asked if there was any way it could get in the house, and I thought it could jump through a window. The kids were scared to death, so I decided to get the 30-30 down."

"You know you're not supposed to touch that gun."

"I had to do something, didn't I? I couldn't let it get in here and hurt the kids."

"Where did you get the shells?"

"I remembered seeing two shells in Mama's sewing drawer." machine

"You were never allowed to get into my sewing machine drawers," Mary said.

"I needed a safety pin for Benny's pants. He couldn't go around all day with his pants always falling down," Johnny said. "I figured you wouldn't want the panther to kill us all, so I got the gun down, got the shells and sat down on the bench to load it. I put the two shells into the breach. Pat, Bobby, Cam and Benny were sitting on the floor in front of me. Bobby was sitting behind the others.

"I can't remember putting a round in the firing chamber, only in the breach. I don't know how the gun went off. The only thing I can figure is that the hammer was back just far enough that when my arm or hand accidentally hit it, it went off."

Ephriam needed more details. "What happened after the gun went off?"

"I looked at the kids sitting there on the floor. They all looked okay, but I asked if anybody was hit, and no one answered. I looked at Bobby and his eyes were as big as saucers, then I could see that his leg had been hit. I asked him if it hurt, and he said no, but I put him on my back and ran to the CCC camp, holding his leg tight against me, trying to stop the bleeding as much as I could."

"What happened there?" Mary's voice was weak.

"The doctor took care of Bobby and then gave me a shot to calm me down. He couldn't believe that I ran all that way with Bobby on my back. The doctor did all he could to take care of Bobby, but he knew that they had to get him to the hospital in Colusa as soon as possible. They had to use one of the CCC trucks as an ambulance. After that shot the doctor gave me, everything was kind of fuzzy, but me and the kids walked back home after the truck left."

Ephriam turned to Pat, Cam and Benny, who were sitting on the bench and fidgeting.

"Is Johnny telling the truth?"

The three nodded.

"Mama, fix these kids something to eat, so they can get to bed," Ephriam said.

"I can't stay here not knowing how Bobby is. We've got to go to him," Mary said.

"It would take us hours to get there in this storm. The roads are too bad. We'll wait up for Jim and then we'll leave early in the morning."

Around three O'clock in the morning, Jim came and let Ephriam and Mary know that Bobby was doing as well as could be expected and was sleeping when he left.

The next morning Johnny went with his parents to the Colusa hospital where two reporters awaited them. Mary told them that they were going to visit Bobby and would talk to them later. When the family finished their visit, the reporters asked them questions and wanted to take some pictures of them. The reporters told them how to pose and began to place them in positions.

Johnny became irate. "Don't you touch me! You're not going to tell me where to stand," he yelled to a surprised reporter, who backed away. But, after a stern look from his mother, Johnny complied and a picture was taken.

When the *Colusa Sun Herald* came out with their article, it made things worse. No one knew where they got their story, but almost all their information was wrong. They even had Bobby's name down as Fred, and they said that Ephriam and Mary had left all fourteen kids at home. The article said that when Ephriam and Mary got home, they found that Bobby had almost bled to death. These were all lies. Bobby was probably already at the hospital when his parents got home.

The story in the *Sacramento Bee* was the worst. It said:

"There's a place in Lake County, where it overlaps Colusa County, that is a very dangerous area. The kids up there in those mountains play cops and robbers with live ammunition; so if you enter that area, you are doing so at your own risk."

That article made Mary madder than hell. She wrote to all the newspapers and told them they were wrong, but none of them acknowledged that they had made any mistakes.

BARKERSVILLE BRIEFS

BARKER HAS YOUTH LEG AMPUTATED

Bobby Barker returned home last Tuesday from the Colusa Memorial Hospital where he had his leg amputated two weeks ago. Bobby was accidentally shot through the leg three years ago and the doctors have tried to save his leg ever since- without success. Bobby feels fine and returned to school Monday.

The only thing they had right was that the bullet struck about four inches below the knee and took a downward course, fracturing several bones in the leg.

The doctors tried to save Bobby's leg. Two of the doctors said the leg would have to come off, but there was one who insisted that it shouldn't be amputated, so they didn't take it off.

Bobby was in the hospital a lot during the next couple of years for bone grafting. They eventually had to amputate the leg and did so when he was fourteen.

One time, while Bobby was still in the hospital, Ephriam and Mary went down to visit him, and left Johnny in charge of the kids again. Pat decided to go hunting for rabbits, so he sneaked the twenty-two single shot out of the house. He went off down the hill, but came limping back soon after.

He came up to Johnny, his face ashen. "I shot myself in the foot."

Johnny knew how it happened. Pat would always put the gun barrel on his foot to cock the gun.

"Why don't you shoot the other one to even things out?" Johnny asked, knowing he was in big trouble — again.

"Should I pour some kerosene on it?" Pat asked.

"Mama might get mad if you waste the kerosene on your stupid foot," Johnny said.

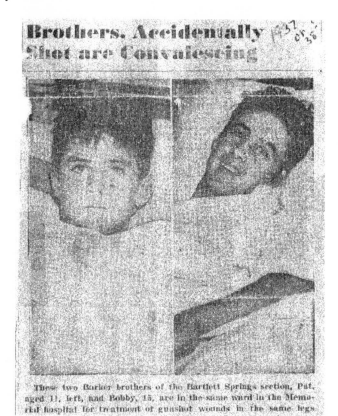

Brothers, Accidentally Shot are Convalescing

These two Barker brothers of the Bartlett Springs section, Pat, aged 11, left, and Bobby, 15, are in the same ward in the Memorial hospital for treatment of gunshot wounds in the same legs.

Johnny wrapped his foot as tightly as he could with his t-shirt and took him to the CCC Camp. The doctor cleaned the wound and wrapped his foot.

Johnny wanted to take him home, but the doctor said he would keep him there until Ephriam picked him up. He said he had to report what happened to the authorities.

Ephriam ended up taking Pat to the hospital, and they put him in the same room with Bobby. Those smart-ass reporters were at it again with the questions and taking pictures. Now it really looked like what they had claimed about playing cops and robbers with live ammunition was true.

Some people believed the story about playing cops and robbers. Even some in his family doubted Johnny's version of the incident.

A Stormy Night — A Tragic End

In February of 1938, fifteen-years-old **Johnny** was told by his mother that he was to go to the stage stop and pick up provisions that would be coming on the stage from the valley. She said that the creek was overflowing its banks and he would have to ford it. The storm was bad. It had rained for thirty-seven days and nights.

Johnny started out about ten in the morning and stopped by the Saylor's place as his mother had asked him to do. They always checked with Mrs. Saylor to see if she needed anything. Her husband was working out of the area and didn't make it home very often.

When Johnny arrived at her house, she was there with her two youngest children, Alafair, who was about seven, and Roy, a couple of years older.

"Do you need anything?" Johnny asked.

"I'm expecting some provisions from the valley, and some money in the mail from my husband."

"I'll pick it up for you then," Johnny said.

"I'll go with you. There's no way you'll be able to carry it all."

Johnny didn't want her to go with him, but she insisted, and they started on their way. The bridge was out so they would have to cross the creek on a pine tree that had fallen across it during a previous storm. They got to the tree and found it completely covered by swiftly moving water.

"Are you sure you can make it across?" Johnny asked. Mrs. Saylor looked tired.

Mrs. Saylor nodded. "

Johnny had to hold onto her and almost lost his grip several times. She was completely exhausted by the time they reached the other side.

"I can't go any farther. Go on to the stage stop. I need to rest awhile," Mrs. Saylor said.

Johnny gave her his rain gear and made her as comfortable as possible, and then went to the Portman ranch and picked up as much of the provisions as he could carry.

When Johnny got back to where he had left Mrs. Saylor, she was still not able to walk.

Her voice was weak. "I don't think I have enough strength to get back."

"I'm going to go to Kowalski's to get a horse, then come back for you," Johnny said. He was scared. She was still extremely weak.

He put her on a log as far back in the bushes as he could get her, and hurried as fast as the storm would let him to Kowalski's place. Kowalski gave Johnny a horse, and he fought his way through the inclement weather that had worsened to a snowstorm. The storm got so bad that he couldn't see where he was going, and he had to stop until it eased.

When he got back to Mrs. Saylor, she was so weak that she couldn't even stand. He tried every way he could to get her on the horse but just couldn't do it. He was tired from fighting the weather and she was like dead weight.

"I have to go back and get help, Mrs. Saylor. I'll hurry back as fast as I can." Johnny had never felt so helpless in his life, and he had a sick feeling inside when he left her.

He got to Kowalski's and told him that he couldn't get Mrs. Saylor on the horse.

Kowalski said he would get a mule and go back with Johnny. He tied the mule to the horse so they wouldn't get separated, and they braved the weather back to Mrs. Saylor.

When they got to the place where Johnny thought he had left her, she was nowhere around. They searched all up and down the area. Johnny was completely confused. He knew she was too weak to get up and walk.

"We're going to have to get some more men. We have to find her soon," Mr. Kowalski said.

Back at his place, Kowalski got some neighbors together and they organized a search party. They wouldn't let Johnny go with them. He was exhausted and shivered from the cold. Mr. Kowalski insisted that he go to bed and get some rest.

Mrs. Kowalski fixed a bed for him, and he slept until Mr. Kowalski's talking awakened him.

WOMAN LOSES LIFE IN STORM IN MOUNTAINS

Mrs. Lela Mary Saylor, 50, Found Dead By Searching Party On Bartlett— Exertion And Exposure Responsible For Death

Weakened by exertion and chilled by rain soaked clothing and low temperature weather during the raging rain and snow storm in the Bartlett mountain section on Wednesday night last week near the Lake-Colusa line, Mrs. Lela Mary Saylor, 50-year-old mother and housewife, residing near Hough Springs, died from exposure while huddling alone in a brush thicket waiting for a rescue party that failed to find her until after death had ensued. Her body was found at 1:30 Thursday morning.

The fate of the unfortunate woman saddened the mountain neighbors who did their utmost to reach her when the alarm had been given them; that she had become exhausted while endeavoring to make her way on foot to the Portman home to obtain provisions that had been sent her from Williams and which she had ordered sent on the stage. She was accompanying young Johnnie Barker, 14-year-old neighbor youth, when she became exhausted in the storm swept mountains.

The fatal mishap occurred across the border line in Colusa county and according to news accounts in the Colusa newspapers and statements of Colusa authorities, Mrs. Saylor and the youth started from the Saylor home, at 10:00 o'clock on Wednesday morning afoot. They had passed the Frank Kowalski place in Indian valley, about three miles from the Saylor home; and then crossed the creek which was too deep to ford in an automobile.

It is stated that Kowalski did not recognize Mrs. Saylor as she was attired in a man's clothing. He would have advised her not to attempt to cross the creek if he had recognized her as the water was too deep and running too swiftly for a woman to endanger herself.

Youth Returns For Horse

Several hours later the youth returned to the Kowalski place and secured a horse so that he could assist Mrs. Saylor who he reported

(Continued on Page 8)

The Road to Barkersville

...EPORT, CALIFORNIA, T

WOMAN LOSES LIFE

(Continued from Page 1).

had become exhausted. He left and then again returned and was exhausted himself. He stated he was unable to lift Mrs. Saylor into the saddle. Kowalski then left with a horse and a mule in company with the youth and when they arrived at the place where the latter had left Mrs. Saylor, she was not to be found. They searched the vicinity in vain and when it became dark Kowalski and young Barker returned to Kowalski's home. Residents of Bear valley were then informed of Mrs. Saylor's disappearance and a searching party was formed and soon started out. The youth was put to bed and was in an exhausted state suffering from cold.

After hours of unsuccessful effort to locate the woman, the party finally came upon her body in Complexion canyon at 1:30 in the morning.

The body was found sitting upright in some bushes on a log. The woman had been endeavoring to protect herself from the elements when death overtook her.

Rescuers stated Mrs. Saylor had evidently been dead for several hours before they found her.

The Searching Party

The searching party was composed of Deputy Sheriff Wilbur Mason of Colusa county, C. Lambert, Frank Boardban and Kowalski.

James Saylor, the woman's husband, has been employed at the Milton D. Dodge ranch below Arbuckle. He was notified of the predicament of his wife when she became lost as was a son, employed at the Paul Cannon Cafe in Williams. It is reported they joined in the search.

Besides her husband and two children, a boy 7 and a girl 9, who lived with her, Mrs. Saylor is survived by four sons by a former marriage. They are William Edwards, Santa Rosa; Dave Edwards, Sacramento; Claude Edwards, Dunnigan; Robert Edwards, president of the senior class in the Williams high school.

Funeral services were held in Colusa on Monday and interment was made in Williams.

Were Homesteaders

The Saylors were on a homestead near Hough Springs. Mrs. Saylor was not of rugged health, it is reported. Coroner J. Deter McNary of Colusa is reported to have stated that it was a case of the woman over-estimating her strength in an effort to make her way through the storm to obtain the provisions that had been left for her by the stage, as well as the mail from Williams.

Sympathy is being expressed in this county for the family in their sadness.

Johnny got up and went into the kitchen where Mr. and Mrs. Kowalski were sitting at the table.

Mrs. Kowalski said, "Johnny, you should go back to bed."

Johnny shook his head. "I have to know about Mrs. Saylor. Was she found?"

"Sit down, Johnny. Mother, get some hot tea," Mr. Kowalski said.

Johnny shook his head again. "I just want to know about Mrs. Saylor."

"We found her about 1:30 this morning in Complexion Canyon."

"Is she all right?" Johnny's stomach knotted. He knew what the answer would be.

"She didn't make it. She was exposed to the cold for too long," Mr.

Kowalski said.

"I shouldn't have let her go with me. God, what will her children do?" Johnny asked. Then he laid his head on the table.

Mr. Kowalski got up and went to him. "I don't think you could have stopped her."

"I gotta get home. Mama will be worried about me."

"Let me fix you some breakfast," Mrs. Kowalski said.

"No, thank you. I can't eat."

"Okay, but eat when you get home." Mrs. Kowalski hugged Johnny, and then he and Mr. Kowalski left.

There was a terrible side effect to that incident, which didn't surprise Johnny. After Mrs. Saylor's death, Johnny had a problem with Jim Saylor. Jim was sure Johnny wasn't being truthful about having to leave Mrs. Saylor behind. He told everyone that a young man as big and strong as Johnny would have been able to get a small woman like Mrs. Saylor on the horse. He accused Johnny of stealing the money that he had sent to his wife. It was assumed by everyone that the letter the money was in got lost in the water. It was never found.

Jim Saylor didn't like Johnny very much anyway, and it might have been because Johnny was always leery of him. Johnny often said that something wasn't right with Jim Saylor, especially after Mrs. Saylor's death, because soon after Mrs. Saylor's death, his daughter started acting in a strange way.

The kids that walked to school with her would see her take off her panties and throw them in the bushes. Teddy would sometimes go get them, stick them in his pocket and give them to her when no one was looking. Well, one day he forgot to do that and came home with them.

Mary saw that Teddy had something in his pocket. "What is that?"

Teddy's face turned red, and he pulled the panties out.

"They're Alafair's. She takes them off and throws them in the bushes when she's walking to school, so I get them and give them back to her. I just forgot today."

"You have been doing this every day? How long has this been going on?" Mary asked.

"Not everyday, maybe once a week. Just ask Pat and Bobby, or Cam. They've seen her too. She's been doing it ever since school started."

Mary knew there was something wrong. That wasn't a normal thing for a little girl to do.

"Did you ask her why she was doing this?"

Pat piped up, "I did, and she said that they were too big and kept falling down."

Mama took the panties from Teddy's hand.

"I don't want you to touch her underwear anymore. I am going to tell Ephriam about this, and he will want to talk to you."

That night Ephriam talked to all of the boys, and he believed they were telling the truth. The next day, he went to have a talk with Jim Saylor, but he wasn't home.

The following day, two state cars came up to the school. Mrs. Nelson, the school teacher, had notified the authorities that Alafair's brother, Roy, had been coming to school dirty and disheveled, and it was happening so often that she was concerned. She told them that when she asked him why, he said that he was sleeping in their doghouse. She asked where his sister was sleeping, and he said with his dad. The day he told her that, she notified the authorities.

They talked a long time with Alafair and Roy, then questioned the boys in school and asked if they were fooling around with Alafair. They said no, but told them that she had been acting strange since her mother died.

Alafair and Roy were put in one of the cars and were taken to the valley, while the remaining officers questioned everyone in the area. When they got to the Barker house, Ephriam told them about the panties and that he had put them in a paper bag and had planned to confront Jim Saylor with them. He gave the bag to them. They asked him what kind of man Jim Saylor was, and Ephriam said he didn't know him too well, as Jim worked out of the area most of the time.

Later that afternoon, the officers went to Jim Saylor's place and arrested him. Jim had been molesting Alafair ever since his wife's death. He got five-to-ten years in prison—not enough in the Barkers' minds. Alafair and Roy went to stay with an older brother that lived in the valley.

Suicide at Mountain House

The Mountain House was an old hotel that sat only a few feet off Leesville Road. It had been closed for business but there was a caretaker that stayed there, an old man who wasn't quite right. He had often been seen going about the place stark naked, talking to himself.

One day, Johnny and Pat were walking up from the valley on their way home, and they stopped at the Mountain House to get some water.

While they walked across the porch, Johnny looked in the window and saw the caretaker slumped over in a chair.

"Pat, come here!" He motioned Pat to the window. "Look at that. There's something wrong with the caretaker."

"Why do you think that?" Pat asked.

"See how he's all slumped over?" Johnny asked, as he pressed his face closer to the glass.

"Maybe he's just sleeping," Pat said.

"Oh, for Christ's sake, he's not sleeping. Something is wrong with him. Let's go inside."

"No way. He hasn't got any clothes on."

"What do you think he's gonna do? Jump up and attack you? Now come on!"

They went into the hotel and when they got close to the old guy, they saw a gruesome sight. The left side of his face was mangled and covered with blood. There was a rifle lying on the floor in front of the chair he was sitting in.

"Jesus, the whole left side of his face has been blown away. Somebody has murdered the poor bastard," Johnny said.

They left in a hurry and continued on their way. They stopped at the first house they came to and told the guy there what they had found.

At first, he told them to go on home, but then he changed his mind. The guy thought the sheriff might want to question them.

He took them back to the Mountain House and told them to stay there while he went to notify the sheriff. He said they needed to stay in case someone else came along that might go in and disturb things.

After he left, Johnny and Pat sat on the porch and tried to figure out who would want to murder an old man like that. They wondered if it could have been robbery. Maybe he had valuables or money hidden somewhere in the house. While they were talking, Johnny kept turning around to look at the window like he expected the old man's ghost to come floating through it.

It was near dark when the sheriff and his deputy got there, and the boys were so glad to see them because the darker it got, the creepier the place became.

The sheriff went inside with his deputy, telling the boys they couldn't go with them. He told them they could wait in his car if they wanted, so they did.

When they were in the car, Pat got a worried look on his face.

"What if they think we killed that guy?"

"Why would they think that? We were the ones that reported it, and we sure as hell wouldn't have if we were guilty." But Johnny had thought about that, too.

The ambulance pulled up and the coroner was in it, along with the attendants. They went inside and came out a little later with the body, which they put in the ambulance.

After they left, the sheriff posted something on the door, and then he and his deputy got in the car, which made Johnny real nervous.

The boys were questioned, but not for long, and the sheriff wouldn't tell them what he thought had happened. He said he would know after the coroner did his report.

Later, it was determined that the caretaker had committed suicide by pushing the trigger with his big toe. He never left a note or anything, and they couldn't find a living relative to notify.

Into a Strange Darkness

When Johnny was seventeen years old, he went with a friend to San Francisco to visit the friend's family. They were only supposed to visit for a couple of days, but the friend decided he wanted to stay longer, so Johnny started to hitchhike back to Barkersville. He was on the highway with his thumb up, when a Rolls Royce limousine with two men inside pulled up beside him. The driver was a young black man wearing a chauffeur's uniform. The other man was sitting in the back seat, and he looked to be about fifty. He was wearing a dark blue suit. He stuck his head out of the window and called to Johnny.

"You want a lift?"

Johnny walked over to the car. The man looked even older close up; he was squinting, making the lines around his eyes look cavernous, and his eyes were badly bloodshot.

"Sure," Johnny said.

The man opened his door and scooted over, so Johnny climbed in beside him.

"Thanks a lot. It's pretty hot out there," Johnny said.

The car was filled with a sickening odor—a mixture of stale cigarettes and dead fish. The man offered Johnny a cigarette, and Johnny shook his head. He lit one for himself, took a few puffs and then snuffed it out. He offered Johnny his hand and introduced himself.

"You can call me J.W."

"I'm John Barker."

"Are you related to Lex Barker?"

"I don't think so."

Johnny was uneasy about the way J.W. was looking at him.

•

The Homestead

They were several miles out of town when J.W. gave the driver an order. "Isaac, turn the car around."

Johnny didn't like that. "Let me out before you do, so I can catch another ride."

"We're just going back to get something to eat, then we'll continue on our way. I'm famished, and I know old Isaac is too. What about you, Johnny? You've got to be hungry. I've never met anyone your age who wasn't."

Johnny was starving. He hadn't eaten since early that morning and now it was close to four in the afternoon. "I could eat a little something."

They went to eat at a dining room in a very swank hotel. The driver left soon after they got there. He said he was going to see someone and would be back in about an hour.

Johnny felt out of place in his Levis and t-shirt, but no one noticed him. They centered their attention on J.W. and gave him the royal treatment. Everyone seemed to know him, and he was very friendly with everyone, even the waiters.

Johnny looked at prices on the menu and almost fell off his chair. And there were so many items to choose from, some he had never heard of. He couldn't make up his mind.

"Let me order for you, Johnny," J. W. said. He motioned to the waiter.

Johnny had prime rib for the first time in his life. It was the best thing he had ever tasted, and he never ate so much in his life. He had two desserts — one was with cherries that they lit on fire with a match.

For the first time, he tasted champagne. He didn't care for it all that much. He liked Diego Red, the wine that everyone he knew drank. But J.W. kept filling his glass, so he kept drinking.

J.W. didn't eat much of the fish he had ordered. He just took a few bites, lit a cigarette, and then sat back and watched Johnny eat.

"How do you like your food, Johnny?"

"It's great, right up there with Mama's," Johnny said, not skipping a bite.

J.W. was still looking at Johnny with that creepy stare, but Johnny didn't let it bother him; he was in hog heaven.

"How would you like to eat like this every day?"

"Who wouldn't?"

J.W. lit another cigarette from the one he had been smoking.

"Johnny, do you like movies?"

"Sure I do, but I don't go very often."

"What kind of pictures do you like?"

"I liked most of the ones I've seen. The one I liked the most is *Mutiny on the Bounty*. I really like Clark Gable—he's a great actor."

"He's a great person too, as well as being one of the best actors around. I liked him from the moment I met him."

"You know Clark Gable?"

"Yes, I know many of the stars. I work in Hollywood; I'm a director and have worked with a lot of them."

"No crap? Like who?"

"Gary Cooper, Henry Fonda, Walter Huston, Betty Davis."

About that time, the first dessert arrived; a little cake covered in peaches and whipped cream. J.W. smiled as Johnny tore into it.

"Johnny, would you like to meet those people we were just talking about?"

Johnny's mouth was full so he just nodded.

J.W. motioned for the waiter. "Bring this guy another dessert, the best that you have, and another bottle of champagne, please."

He put his arms on the table and leaned towards Johnny. His bloodshot eyes looked sleepy.

"Johnny, I want you to come back to Hollywood with me. I want to give you a screen test. I think you would be a natural, and I think you're better looking than most of those pansies there now. You have a real manly look about you."

Johnny's eyes bugged out, and he choked on the champagne that he had just taken a swig of.

"You want me to go with you to become an actor? I don't know a damned thing about that kind of stuff. I would be like a fish out of water."

"I'll teach you everything you need to know about the business. There isn't much to being an actor. It wouldn't take you long to learn the ropes."

"I haven't got any money. How would I live?"

"You'd stay with me, and I'd provide everything you'd need. Of course, this would only be until you started earning a decent living."

At first, this seemed ridiculous to Johnny, but the more they talked and the more champagne Johnny drank, the more excited he became.

They had been there for about two hours, and Isaac still hadn't come back. Johnny thought that was strange, but when he mentioned it to J.W., he didn't seem concerned.

The champagne was kicking in, and Johnny was a little woozy. He had been up almost all of the night before, and right about then, he was wishing he had a place to lie down.

J.W. must have read Johnny's mind because he smiled then. "You look like you could use a little rest. I have a place where you can rest for a while."

He got up, and Johnny followed him. After J.W. whispered something to the waiter, they got in the elevator and went up to the 4th floor. The elevator was hot as hell, and Johnny's stomach dropped to the floor as it started up.

They entered a room that was bigger than a lot of the houses Johnny's family had lived in. There were some bottles of liquor sitting on a table, and J.W. went to them and began mixing drinks.

"Johnny, you go take a shower. It'll make you feel better."

Johnny wasn't used to hotel rooms. He had never been in one before, and to be there with a stranger just didn't seem right.

"I just want to rest awhile," he said, flopping down on the sofa.

J.W. went to the closet and brought back a white robe.

"At least take off your things and put this on."

Johnny shook his head. No way was he going to put that robe on. He never had a robe on before, and it didn't seem right to do that either.

J. W.'s voice had a tinge of anger when he spoke. "Go lie on the bed anyway. You need to sleep. I'm going to take a shower." He then went into the bathroom, taking the robe and a drink with him.

Johnny knew that he was in a situation that he had to get out of as soon as possible.

His head was still fuzzy. He looked at the bed. It was covered with a light-blue spread and huge, white fluffy pillows. Heaven? It sure did look like that to Johnny. It beckoned him until he couldn't resist, and he went and sunk his head into one of those clouds.

He figured that he could sleep for a minute or two before J.W. got out of the shower.

He was a light sleeper, and he was sure he would wake up when J.W. came back into the room. He was wrong. He awoke hours later to find the room dark, with only a sliver of light coming through the narrow part in the drapes. At first, he was confused and thought that he was in his bed at home, but after a minute, he remembered where he was.

He just wanted to get out of there, and he started to get up.

"Where are you going, Johnny?" J.W. asked in a soft, sickening tone. Then he grabbed Johnny and pulled him back down on the bed.

Before Johnny could get back up, J.W. jumped on top of him. Johnny was just going to throw him off, but when he felt J.W.'s nakedness, he was so repulsed that he hit him in the face with all his might. J.W. crumpled to the floor, and Johnny jumped up, fumbled for the light switch and turned the lights on.

J.W. was out cold. There was blood all over his face and his nose was smashed. His milky-white body looked like a corpse.

Johnny didn't know if he should go get someone or just leave. He decided J.W. was probably going to be all right and that someone would be checking on him soon.

Johnny snuck down the stairs and walked back to where his friend was. It was so spooky walking all that way, and he barely made it, he was so tired. It would be two more days before his friend could take him back home, and Johnny sweated those days, thinking he might have killed J.W. He looked in the newspaper to see if there was anything about J.W. There wasn't, and he breathed a little easier.

A few weeks later, Johnny got a letter from J.W. It was easy to write to someone on a star route by just putting a name, star route, and the town and state.

J.W. apologized to Johnny. He said that he didn't mean any harm, and that he was just horsing around, the way Johnny must have horsed around with his brothers. Johnny couldn't believe he said such a repulsive thing, because he had never met anybody in his life who would wrestle around naked with their brothers. He also said that any time Johnny wanted to have that screen test, he would send his driver for him, and that if Johnny wanted, he could bring a couple of his brothers with him.

He said that he forgave Johnny for hitting him, and that he had to have surgery on his nose.

Johnny threw the letter away. He didn't want any part of Hollywood. If there were people like J.W. there, it couldn't be a good place. It seemed the price of fame was just too high—for Johnny anyway.

The Wrong Turn

It all started in October of 1945, when Bobby's girl, Mary Gash, told him she didn't want to see him anymore. On one of their dates, he'd gotten drunk and kept her out all night against her will. It was only one of many reasons for breaking up with him.

Bobby always got drunk. He didn't do anything without booze. He had taken his first drink when he was fourteen years old, when Johnny had come up to Barkersville with a bottle of wine. He took a few drinks then, but that started him on the road to becoming an alcoholic. Everybody told him that he was an alcoholic, and he had to agree because he couldn't stop at just a couple of drinks, he had to keep going until he got dead drunk.

About a week after Mary broke up with him, Bobby couldn't stand it anymore. He wrote a letter telling Mary that he loved her more than anything else in the world. He told her that if he lost her, he would be losing everything, and that he couldn't stand not seeing her. He begged her to write back, begged her to forgive him.

Bobby waited for a couple of weeks, and when he didn't hear from Mary, he tried to see her, but her mother wouldn't let him. He had lost her, and he couldn't eat, sleep or work. He didn't know what to do, but he did know that whatever he did, he would be doing it while drunk, because all he wanted to do was pour the booze down.

Near the end of November, he and Pat left Fruto, where the family was living at the time, to go to Colusa. That's where Mary Gash lived and **Bobby** wanted to try once more to see her, before giving up for good.

It didn't work. Mary's mother told him that Mary wasn't home and would be gone for a few days. He didn't believe her. *Fine*, he thought, *I won't try to see her or contact her anymore.*

He and Pat wandered around town and ended up getting a couple of bottles of wine and going to the park. They did this almost every time they went to Colusa. They were just finishing up the wine and wondering how they were going to get back home when they saw Gerald Gallego, a friend of theirs, drive by. They yelled and waved for him to stop, and he pulled over.

They were glad to see him. Even though Gerald Gallego was of questionable character, he was always a lot of fun to be around, and at that time, Bobby needed someone like him to distract him from his hopeless problems. Gallego loved to drink as much as Pat and Bobby did, and most of time, he had booze with him.

"What the hell are you guys doing here?" Gallego asked.

"Long story," Bobby said.

"What about you?" Pat asked.

"I'm on my way back to Broderick where I live now. I've been visiting my uncle over in Williams."

"We're trying to get home ourselves," Bobby said.

"Still living in Fruto?" Gallego asked.

"Yeah, and we really need a ride. Can you take us?" Bobby said.

"If you buy the gas and whiskey."

"Take us over to the store," Pat said and grinned.

Inside the store, Bobby approached the counter, the whiskey in one hand and a checkbook in the other. The clerk looked hard at Bobby, as if sizing up his trustworthiness. Bobby should have been worried about having enough in his account, but the more he drank, the less he worried.

They filled up the car and started to Fruto. When they got there, they sat in the car for a couple of hours, talking and drinking whiskey until Gallego said that he needed to start home. Gallego was in no shape to drive, so Bobby told him he'd better stay and leave early the next morning. He agreed, and they sat in the car until about three in the morning when Gallego told Bobby and Pat to get out. He was leaving for home.

They tried to talk him into sleeping for a while, but he wouldn't listen. He kept telling them to get out of the car. They wouldn't do it. He got angry and took off really fast. When he tried to make the corner at the end of the road, he rolled the car. It rolled twice and landed back on its wheels. They weren't hurt, just shaken up.

Gallego tried starting the car. It wouldn't start, and he became upset. "Jesus Christ! What am I going to do?"

"Let's wait. Then we'll try again," Pat said.

Gallego laid his head on the steering for a couple of minutes then tried again.

"Damn, damn, damn! What am I going to do?" Gallego said.

"Bobby can probably fix your car," Pat said.

"This ain't my car," Gallego said.

Bobby and Pat exchanged a look. What had they gotten into?

"Whose is it?" Bobby asked.

"I don't know. I took it from a neighbor of my uncle's," Gallego said.

"What?" Bobby asked.

"You heard right. I took the damned thing. I got mad at my aunt who was giving me hell for my drinking, so I took off walking. I saw a car turning out of a driveway, and I put my thumb out, but they didn't pick me up. That made me madder than hell. So I walked down that driveway to the house, and when I saw this car parked there, I had the urge to take it, so I hotwired it."

"Almighty Christ! This is a stolen car," Pat said, and then he got out of the car.

"I'm going back to the house; this is bullshit."

"We've got to think about this," Bobby said.

"Think about what? I don't want to get mixed up in this. I don't want to go back to the pen."

Pat had spent time in Preston a year before, and Bobby didn't want him to get in trouble again, either. He had gotten a bad rap with that deal and everyone thought it was unfair. What happened was that he was out riding around one night with their brother Johnny and a friend, Frank Bond, when they ran out of gas. They went into somebody's barn and were siphoning gas from one of the farm machines; it was dark so **Pat** lit a match so they could see better. That caused an explosion in the gas tank, which started a fire. The guys were able to get out safely but the barn was damaged. Well, they were arrested, and Johnny and Frank got out of it because they had gotten draft notices, but Pat was convicted and sent to Preston School of Industry. Pat felt he should have gotten probation, as that was his first offense, and especially since the other two, who were older, were not charged at all.

"You ain't going to prison, Pat. We've got to take this car some place and hide it," Gallego said, and then he tried to start the car.

The car started right up. Pat got back inside, and they took off again.

Pat and Bobby should have gone back home right then, but they were pretty well lit, and their mother hated them coming home like that. Besides, they weren't ready to stop drinking.

"Where are we going?" Bobby asked.

"I guess to Broderick," Gallego said.

Bobby lit a cigarette and handed it to Gallego.

"Give me one too," Pat said.

Bobby gave Pat a cigarette and then lit one for himself. They were silent for a few minutes.

"Maybe we shouldn't go to your house," Bobby said. The cops

might be on the lookout for the car, and your house is close to the main highway. "

Pat spoke up from the back. "Let's go to Lodoga. Edith will let you put the car in the barn until you can think of what you're going to do. And, there shouldn't be any cops on those roads."

It was about five in the morning when they arrived at Edith's place. They slept in the car until about eight, when Edith's husband, Bill, woke them up.

"What in the hell happened to this car?" Bill asked.

"Got into a little bang up last night; Insurance will fix it up," Gallego said.

"Looks like you all could use some coffee; Come on in. Edith just made some," Bill said.

They went into the house and had coffee, and after Gallego told how the car got banged up, Bobby asked Edith if it would be all right if Gallego kept his car in the barn for a few days until he could get the insurance company to fix it. He hated to lie, but he couldn't involve them.

Edith agreed, and they began moving the car into the barn.

"Why can't you just leave the car outside?" Bill asked.

"The top's messed up. I don't want rain to get inside the car," Gallego lied.

Edith made them some breakfast, but Bobby couldn't eat much nor could Pat, but Gallego had no problem gobbling down more than his share of potatoes and eggs. Bill had to go to work down in Colusa, so they rode down with him, and he dropped them off in town.

They were out of smokes and out of booze, so they went to the store again. Bobby was glad to see the storekeeper's wife behind the counter this time. He had to write another check, and he didn't want to face the old man's questioning eyes. He bought three bottles of wine, one for each of them, and some cigarettes.

They went to the park, sat under a tree, and drank the wine, still trying to figure out what Gallego should do about the car. They stayed there until one o'clock that afternoon and then walked around town. Bobby wanted to go see Mary but the other guys told him that if he went to her in the condition he was in, she would hate him even more.

While walking past Stokes' machine shop, they stopped to look at Bill Stokes' '41 Chevy he kept parked in the back. It was a neat car, a beauty, and after looking to see if anyone was around, they got inside. Still keeping their wine bottles in the paper bags, they opened them up again and started drinking. Pat dropped his bottle, and it spilled all over the back seat.

"Jesus Christ! I spilled most of my bottle!" Pat said. He had no concern for the seat.

"We don't have anything to clean it with," Bobby said. He opened the glove box to see if there was something there to mop the wine up with. He didn't find anything, but he picked up a key and was looking at it when Gallego grabbed it from his hand.

"Mad Maggie! What do we have here?" He put the key in the ignition.

"Does it fit?" Bobby asked, and Gallego nodded.

"Does what fit?" Pat scooted up and stuck his head in the front seat.

Gallego turned the key, and the car started. He shut it off immediately.

"Jesus, why would anybody leave a key in the glove box? Stupid, just stupid," Pat said, and leaned back in his seat again.

Gallego tapped his fingers on the steering wheel. He tapped for about a minute and then stopped. He looked over at Bobby, who didn't like the look in his eyes. Then Gallego started the car.

"What the in the hell are you doing?" Bobby asked.

"The old man won't even know it's missing. He stays inside that shop until after dark. We'll have it back way before then."

He proceeded slowly out unto the street and turned on a road that led out into the country.

"All right! Let's roll!" Pat said, and that made crazy Gallego push the gas peddle to the floor.

"Wooie! Mad Maggie!" Gallego said, and then laughed like hell.

"Slow down, or I'm going to punch you in the gut!" Bobby said.

"Okay, Bob, damn, don't get violent. I'll slow down some, just for you. But I tell you right now, this car is made for speed." He slowed down and drove out along the river road.

When they got to a place where they could park, Bobby told Gallego to stop so he could take a leak. They all did that, and then stayed there for a while. Bobby made Gallego give his wine to Pat, telling him he couldn't drink any more until he took the car back. Gallego protested, but he knew Bobby meant it.

They started back to town, staying on the road that ran alongside the river. When they were a couple of blocks away from the machine shop, they saw a cop car sitting beside it.

"Holy cow-shit! Cops are there!" Gallego yelled, and then he did a u-turn and headed back the other way.

"Why in the hell did you have to take this damned car? You're a flat-out idiot! We shouldn't have even sat in this car." Bobby didn't know who he was angrier with—Gallego or himself.

"I can't take it back now. Let's just wait until later tonight, and we'll sneak it back," Gallego said as he headed out of town.

"The cops will be hiding and waiting for us," Pat said.

"We've got to ditch it somewhere, and I know a good place to do that," Gallego said.

Bobby wished that he could think of something smart to do, but the alcohol dimmed any common sense that he had. He thought he had no choice but to go along with Gallego's plan.

They ended up in Broderick. Gallego and his wife Lorraine had been living there with his wife's sister, Romaine. It was dark when they got there. When the girls found out about the car, they told the guys to leave. If the cops found the car there, they would all be arrested. And there was probably an all points bulletin out on the car.

"We need to take the car out in the country and ditch it," Gallego said.

They all agreed that it was probably the only thing they could do. Gallego convinced Lorraine to go with them, and Lorraine's sister decided she would go, too.

The car was running low on gas, so they had to take a chance and they went to a gas station, which had a small grocery store. Bobby wrote another check, paying not only for the gas but also for some sandwich stuff and beer. Bobby was nervous about writing those checks. He didn't have a lot of money in his account and had only had it for about a month. He had opened it when he started to work but hadn't put very much money into it.

They were riding along on the back roads eating dry bologna sandwiches and drinking cheap beer, when the name Dick Burnham came up. Dick had been a friend of Gallego's until he'd made a move on Lorraine and was chased out of town with the threat of death. Gallego would get steaming mad whenever he talked about Burnham. Bobby had witnessed that before. He tried to change the subject, but Gallego kept ranting and raving about the no-good Burnham, and started swerving.

"Pull over. You're driving like an idiot," Bobby said.

"I'm driving all right. Besides, I want to go to Ukiah and see what Burnham is up to these days, and I know you won't take me."

"You moron, we can't do that. We have to get rid of this car. Besides you don't know that he's even in Ukiah," Bobby said.

"I know that no-good bum is living there with his parents. He's so damned lazy that he's lived off them most of his life. And we can get rid of the car there, that will be an even better place," Gallego said.

Bobby couldn't force him to stop, because Lorraine was sitting between them.

Pat was in the back seat with Romaine, and she was giggling and telling him to stop whatever he was doing. Bobby glanced back occasionally to tell Pat to knock it off, but that didn't do any good. Pat couldn't keep his hands off any girl that was within his reach.

Bobby was nervous as hell as they headed to Ukiah. He kept looking for cop cars and told everyone else to look, too. They were all tense, and Lorraine said that they should all sing, and she started singing "Rum and Coca Cola." Bobby wasn't in the mood to sing, especially a happy song. He started singing inside his head, "You always hurt the one you love" and that kept popping into his head for the rest of the night.

Bobby's heart was in his throat all the way to Ukiah from watching for cops and watching Gallego's driving. He sighed with relief when they finally pulled into the driveway of a rundown house on the outskirts of town in the early hours of morning. There were lights on inside, and Gallego went to the door and knocked.

"We're dead now. There's going to be trouble," Bobby said.

"Gerald won't do a thing," Lorraine said. "He's backed down from Dick lots of times. He's not about to tackle that huge guy. You just watch, they'll be all buddy, buddy."

The door opened, and Gallego went inside for a few minutes and then came back out to the car with Burnham.

They talked for a bit, and then Gallego said, "Hey, friend, hope there ain't no hard feelings between us; as far as I'm concerned, we'll always be buddies.

"That's right, buddies for life," Burnham said, and the two shook hands.

"We've got a big problem, Dick," Gallego said, shaking his head.

"What kind of problem?" Burnham asked.

"We took this car for a joyride and aimed to take it back, but the cops were waiting when we went to return it."

"You're driving around in a stolen car?" Burnham asked.

"We meant to take it back," Gallego said.

"I think I know where you might be able to pick up another car. There's one that's always parked in back of Jim's Junk store on Center Street. The old man who owns it only drives it once in a while, and the store is on a back street, so you could probably get out of town without being seen," Burnham offered, "and you can ditch this car at the park that's a block down from the store."

"Sounds good," Gallego said. "Hey, come with us. We've got plenty of booze and cigarettes, and we're having a good time."

Gallego had no trouble ditching the stolen car and hot-wiring the 1940 Buick. They crawled out of town. They started having car trouble as soon as they took off. It kept cutting out, and they chugged along, mindful of the fact that they probably wouldn't get too far.

"We're gonna have to find another car," Gallego said "Damn, it's a nice one too; I could get used to driving around in this baby."

"I know a guy in Willets, who might lend me a car and possibly some money," Burnham said.

"Let's go, then." Gallego headed toward Willets, the car sputtering all the way. They barely made it to the guy's house.

Everyone waited in the car while Burnham went inside. He came out later with a chubby bald guy and went over to an old Chevy parked at the side of the house. The car belonged to the chubby guy's father-in-law who was recuperating in the hospital from a heart attack. The car wasn't in bad shape, just old, and the key was in it.

"You can borrow this old thing for a couple of days, but it's gotta be back here by Friday—that's when the old man gets out of the hospital," the chubby man said. He squinted at the car where the rest of the gang waited. "Who ya got with you?"

"Just some friends," Burnham said.

A leering smile spread across the man's large face. "I see some gals in there. Any chance I could borrow one of 'em for a few minutes?"

"Nah, they belong to those fellows."

"Can't blame a feller for tryin', can ya?"

Burnham offered his hand. "Hey, thanks man, I really appreciate your help. Oh, and do you have a couple of bucks I can borrow? I'll pay you back when we bring the car back."

The man brought his wallet out. "I've only got a ten; I ain't got no change."

"Could you get by without it until we get back? I promise, I'll give it back to you then."

"I reckon I can. But ya better pay me back; that's my drinkin' money, and I need it for when I run out."

The ten dollars wasn't going to last long—besides the gas, they needed food and cigarettes. They started on their way, not knowing where they were going. They were discussing how they were going to get more money when Romaine said she knew where she could get some. Alberta Pullen, a friend of hers who lived in Cave Junction, Oregon, owed her money.

"Hell, we can't go to Oregon," Pat piped up. "It'll take all the money we got, and what if she won't give us any once we get there?"

"She owes me money from her last trip to Colusa to visit her folks. I lent her money for a bus ticket back home."

"What the hell good is that gonna do us?" Pat scoffed.

"We'll worry about that when the time comes," Gallego said. "Right now, we've got to get food and gas."

They stopped at a little store and got the same crap to eat—stale bread, bologna, and bad beer—and headed to Cave Junction. It was nice to finally be riding in a car they had permission to be in. For miles, they bellowed, "Don't Fence Me In."

Bobby was less nervous, but always in the back of his mind, he worried about what would happen when they went back home. How had he let himself get caught up in this escapade?

He tried blaming it on Mary. But of course, he knew better than that. He knew he had no one to blame but his sorry-ass self.

They made it to Cave Junction, only having to fill the tank once more, and went to the restaurant where Romaine said her friend worked. They all went in to have some coffee. Romaine didn't see her friend and found out she no longer worked there.

"So now we're stuck. Any other bright ideas?" Bobby said, disgusted.

"I have the address where she lives. It's not too far from here," Romaine said, and Gallego agreed.

They pulled up to a boarding house. Romaine and Lorraine went in to see if Alberta was there. Shortly after, Lorraine came out and motioned the guys inside.

Inside the small room, Romaine was sitting on a sofa beside a pretty blonde girl, who got up when the guys came in and introduced herself.

"Where have you been all my life, beautiful?" Pat took Alberta's hand and kissed it. Pat was always the charmer.

Alberta giggled. "Would y'all like some coffee and something to eat?"

They were starved. She fixed pancakes and coffee, and Bobby let himself relax a bit. He had been tied up in knots for the past few days, and it felt good to unwind.

Alberta was a pleasant girl, and she was obviously enjoying their company.

"You guys are welcome to stay here. I'm off work for the next four days for the Thanksgiving holiday."

"We can't stay," Burnham said. "I promised to get the old man's car back by Friday."

"Oh, come on, please stay," Alberta begged. "My roommate is gone and I'll be here all alone. You have to eat Thanksgiving dinner some place, and I'm a great cook."

"We can't leave a beautiful girl like this alone on Thanksgiving, now can we?" Pat winked at Alberta and put his arm around her.

"We can stay for dinner tomorrow, but that's it," Burnham said.

Bobby didn't have a problem with staying. At least they would have a dinner. He was going to miss having Thanksgiving dinner at home, though. No one could cook turkey, or anything else, like his mother could. He wondered what she would think if she knew what they were doing.

They went to the store with Alberta and helped her pick out a turkey. They had a good time. Alberta was a lot of fun to be around and was always wisecracking. She bought some rum and cola and fixed them a supper that night of hot dogs and macaroni salad.

They listened to music on Alberta's phonograph, and she had a lot of good music. But the song that got played more than the others was "Sentimental Journey." After a few glasses of the rum and cola, that song seemed to fit the mood they were all in.

Alberta had twin beds in her bedroom, and her sofa could be made into a bed. Around eleven o'clock, Alberta made the sofa up, which she said three of the guys could sleep on, and one would have to sleep on the floor. She said the two girls could share her roommate's bed.

They were all tired, and by twelve, everyone turned in, except Pat and Alberta. Gallego, Dick and Bobby were sleeping on the couch, and Alberta was sitting in the chair across the room from them. Pat was sitting next to her chair on the bed she had made for him on the floor.

Alberta turned the light out and they sat quietly for a few moments. Then Pat whispered, "Hey, let's go out to the car so we can talk. We don't want to disturb anybody in here."

"They are all pretty tired. I guess we could go out for a while," Alberta said softly.

They quietly exited the house.

The next morning, the girls got up early and were chattering away in the kitchen. Bobby was hung over. Cola and rum always did that to him, but after four cups of coffee, he felt a lot better.

Alberta got the turkey in the oven, and the other girls made pies. The guys played cards, and after a while, the great smell of the cooking turkey permeated the air. It was almost a normal Thanksgiving Day, and they were all in high spirits. They had a great dinner, after which Burnham said they had to get on the road.

Gallego, Dick, Bobby and the girls were ready to leave, but they had to wait for Pat, who had gone into the bedroom with Alberta. After about a half hour, Pat came out.

"Let's get out of here," Burnham said, heading for the door.

"We have to wait until Alberta throws a few things in a bag," Pat said to everyone's surprise.

"Why would Alberta want to go with us? There's no room, and how will she get back?" Bobby asked, knowing it had to be Pat's idea. He could get a woman to follow him anywhere.

Just as Bobby finished speaking, Alberta came out and said, "I hope you don't mind if I come along with you guys. I have money for gas and stuff, and I have enough for a bus ticket back."

That settled it. They had to take her—she was the one with the money, and it would've been rude to ask to borrow it after that.

They all piled in the car. Burnham drove, Gallego and Loraine got in front with him, and Pat, Alberta, Romaine, and Bobby squeezed in the back.

They stopped a lot to get out and stretch, so the ride to Willits took longer than usual. They talked about what they would do after taking the car back and how they would get back home. Alberta suggested they take a bus, but they didn't have money for that.

They arrived at the house where they were to return the car around midnight. They all got out of the car and went to the door. Burnham knocked several times, but there was no answer. They took turns knocking, but no one came to the door. Lights were on in the house, and the window shades were up, but no one could be seen inside.

"What do we do now?" Bobby asked, shivering in his shirtsleeves. "It's colder than hell out here."

"Let's see if we can get inside," Gallego said as he tried the doorknob.

"Yeah, they won't care; they wouldn't want us to stay out here in the cold," Burnham said.

Bobby was uneasy. "I don't think we should do that."

"Me neither. We should wait. They're probably just out for a while," Alberta said.

"They won't mind. Dick is their friend. No one would want a friend to stay out in the cold and freeze," Loraine said.

"I'm gonna see if there's a window open," Pat said, and he found one that was on the side of the house facing the street that was unlocked. He called to the others, "Come on! We can get in through this one."

Bobby had a bad feeling as Pat went through the window. The rest followed him. Just as it was his turn to go through, red lights flashed from two patrol cars coming up the driveway. Bobby froze where he stood.

Each car had two cops, and they had their guns in their hands when they exited the cars. Bobby's heart fell. They were going to be arrested, and the charges would be serious.

Burnham, Pat and the girls came out of the house, but Gallego stayed inside.

Burnham came up to Bobby and whispered in his ear. "Gallego found a rifle in the house. He said he's going down shooting."

Bobby's heart, which had been in his stomach, was now in his feet, and he suddenly became nauseated at the thought of being involved in killing cops.

The officers slowly approached them. When they got close, Burnham greeted them and tried to shake hands, but one of them told them to put their hands up and line up against the wall of the house.

The cops searched them and asked if there was anyone in the house. None of them answered, and two of the cops started toward the front door.

"Wait …officers!" Bobby called to them, "There's someone in there, and he might have a gun."

One of the officers went around to the back of the house, and the two that were at the front door, kicked the door open.

"Come out with your hands up, or we're going to come in shooting!" the older of the two officers said.

"Okay, I'm coming out with my hands up!"

The officers at the front door stood back, and Gallego came out with his hands in the air.

The cops quickly grabbed him, handcuffed his hands behind him, and placed him under arrest. The officers led him out and took him to a patrol car. They shoved him into the back of the car, hitting his head hard against the top of the door opening.

Another officer placed the others under arrest and cuffed Pat, Burnham and Bobby. The girls were not cuffed. Pat, Lorraine and Romaine were put in the car that had Gallego, and Alberta was put with

The Homestead

Burnham and Bobby.

On the way to the jail, Bobby got sicker, and they had to pull over to let him throw up. The officer that helped him out of the car thanked him.

"You might have saved our lives, and I commend you for that. I don't think any of the others would have done that. You should feel good about yourself for doing the right thing."

But Bobby didn't feel good about anything. He was so down that he thought he was going to die. He felt responsible for the situation that Pat was in. He started thinking about his mother, and that brought tears to his eyes. There he was, a grown man, crying for his mother.

When they got to the police station in Ukiah, the gang was questioned individually before they were booked and put in a cell. Alberta cried her head off, and Pat looked scared and dazed. Lorraine was worried more about her husband than herself, and Romaine just looked tired.

When they questioned Bobby, he told them what had taken place, starting from the time they took Stokes' car right up to the time they were arrested. He didn't tell them about the car they took to Lodoga, but they already knew about that; Gallego must have told them. Bobby told them that none of the girls were involved with any of the stuff they did, and he tried to make it easy on Pat.

At their preliminary hearing, Pat, Bobby, Gallego and Burnham were charged with three counts of car theft and passing bad checks. The girls were released because all the guys said they were not involved in taking the cars.

While Bobby and Pat waited for trial, Ephriam and Cam came for a visit, and Bobby finally got the news he was longing to hear. Cam told him that Mary said that she wanted to come see him, and said that the next time someone came to visit, he would make sure they brought Mary. That lifted Bobby's spirits, and even though he was locked up and facing prison, he had something to live for again.

On the next visiting day, Edith brought Mary with her. Mary cried when Bobby walked into the visiting room. They grabbed each other, and Bobby began crying, too.

"Bobby, I'm sorry, so sorry," Mary said between sobs.

"It's okay, baby, I don't blame you. It was my fault. I love you so much, and I'll never do anything to hurt you again, ever."

"I'm going to write to you every day," Mary said.

"Mary, when I get out of here, will you marry me? Please give me something to look forward to."

Mary nodded. "Yes, I will."

Bobby and Pat were each sentenced to several months in San Quentin, and Bobby was almost glad that he was going to have to pay for what he'd done, because then his slate would be clean, and he could start a new life with Mary.

Although happy about Mary, Bobby wasn't happy about how he had hurt his mother and younger bothers and sisters, who had always been so happy to see him. He had let them down, and he vowed he would make it up to his family when he got out of San Quentin.

Doing time in Quentin wasn't all that bad. There were some good guys in there who'd just had a run of bad luck. A guy named Mack severely beat up a cop and left him at a dump. He had found out that the cop was sneaking in the bedroom window of his thirteen-year-old daughter at night when Mack was at work. Mack tried to have him arrested, but the cop denied it, and the authorities said there wasn't any proof. Mack's daughter wouldn't say if it was true, because the cop had threatened to take her away from her family if she did. Mack said he had left that creep at the right place—garbage belonged in a dump.

Ephriam and Mary took the little kids to see Bobby and Pat a couple of times, and that pleased Bobby so much. He loved being around kids, especially his brothers and sisters, and they were happy to see him. He told them that they'd better not end up in a prison, and that they would have to deal with him if they did. Charlie, who was five, wanted to know if he had to sleep and eat with handcuffs on, and if they could keep dogs with them.

Mary Gash wrote to Bobby often, and their letters to each other were filled with hope and anticipation of getting married and living happily ever after. Bobby made a vow not to drink any more. He wouldn't take a chance of ruining his life, again.

Bobby got time off for good behavior and was released on parole Dec. 9, 1946. His father picked him up. Although he wanted to see Mary that first night, he knew he had to go home and spend some time with his family first. He saw Mary the next night. His father took him to pick her up, and then he dropped them off at the Chinese restaurant in Colusa.

They had dinner and talked for about three hours. They got funny looks from the other people there when they kissed several times, but they didn't care. Cam was supposed to pick them up, but they couldn't wait any longer; they had to find a place to be alone together. It was cold out, but they took off walking and ended up at the park.

Bobby talked his mother into letting Mary come up and stay with them. He would be working with his father and wouldn't be able to see her very often. He told his mother that he and Mary were going to get married as soon as he could save up a little money. So she said if that was the case, it'd be all right, but only if the girls agreed to have her sleep in their room. The girls agreed because they adored Mary.

Mary came up and stayed, but a few days later, her mother sent someone to bring her back home. Bobby tried to talk her out of going, but his mother said that it was the best thing to do, that Mary shouldn't go against her mother. So Mary left, and Bobby was lonely again, but he had the consolation of knowing that they would be married soon.

Bobby saw Mary as often as he could, but it wasn't enough for him. Around the middle of March, Bobby talked her into coming back up to his house, and his mother agreed, again, so at the end of March, Mary rode up with the mailman and stayed with Bobby's family until she and Bobby were married.

Bobby and Mary had problems in their marriage from the start. The vow Bobby had made to stop drinking was soon broken. Once more he turned to booze to ease his burdens. Mary tried her best to make things good, but Bobby would slip into his melancholy mood; he just couldn't seem to help himself. He should've been happy about how things were going for him, but deep inside, he had the crazy idea that he didn't deserve to be happy.

In February of 1948, Bobby and Mary's first child was born—a beautiful baby girl—and now he had two people to take care of. That scared Bobby, because he wasn't doing a very good job of taking care of one, much less two. But in spite of those worries, his baby girl made him happier than he had ever been in his life. However, he and happiness were never able to keep company for too long before something bad would happen, and it did, a few months later on August 18, 1948, when his mother died. That tore the heart out of him. He began drinking more than ever and caused more pain for his wife.

Bad luck Bobby didn't live long after his mother died; on February 19, 1950, he accidently shot himself in the chest while pulling a loaded shotgun from the backseat of his car while out hunting with his wife and daughters. He was twenty-six years old.

Suicide Mission

When a terrible storm or flood would happen in Indian Valley and the family couldn't get out to town, they would get what supplies they could from Mrs. Abel at Hough Springs. She kept an extra supply of food on hand for people to buy if they couldn't get out to town.

During one of those times, Ephriam said to **Teddy**, "You and Pat have to come with me to the Abel's place. I need to pick up some food there."

They walked all the way up to the big oak that was on the bank of the big swimming hole. There were two cables, side-by-side, about a foot apart, going across the creek there.

"I think it would be better if you boys go by yourselves. Those cables might not support me. I'll wait here for you. Mrs. Abel will be expecting you and she'll have some sacks for you."

Teddy looked at the cables, then at his father with fear in his eyes.

"You boys have to go across here, just be careful."

The wooden step that used to be there had fallen to the bottom, and the two cables were twisted around each other, but the boys knew they had to cross.

Teddy looked at Pat, to see if he was as scared as he was; but he looked calm as could be. Pat always had nerves of steel.

Ted prayed, "Oh Lord, just help us get across this thing."

They made it across and Mrs. Abel gave them each a sack, which they tied over one shoulder, then filled them with groceries. It was a wonder that they ever made it back across.

During one of those storms, Teddy lost two pet coons, Jim and Jenny, that he'd had for two years. He had built them a house on some logs by the creek, and the water got so high that it took them, along with their house. He used to trap coons; that's how he got those two for pets. He would go with his father to sell the furs to a guy in Sacramento, and to Sears and Roebuck, and would always make enough to buy a shirt or pants.

Teddy never bought shoes, though. He would make shoes out of old tires. He didn't make a lot because they were hard to do, and the tires were hard to come by. Tires weren't like they are now; they didn't have plies.

Seaton Jr., or "Bugs", as he was called, a cousin who lived up in Barkersville, begged Teddy to make a pair of those shoes for him, but Teddy never would. It was because Seaton was always killing bugs. He had to kill every bug that he saw, and Teddy didn't like that at all. His family was taught to never kill anything for the fun of it, and to only fish or hunt animals when they were needed for food or for selling.

Dangerous Games

The kids had a lot of fun up there, but some of their games were dangerous. They would roll down the hills by the house in barrels and tires, and sometimes the barrel would take somebody to the canyon, where they would end up bleeding somewhere on their body. Pat would always ride to the bridge; he was a daredevil. Sometimes, the other kids wondered if he was all there.

When the three Cs opened the trail above the Saylor's, it became their best runway. One time Pat tried to make a sled to go down the hills on. Well, he made it all right except for one thing; he put one runner pointing one way, and the other pointing the opposite. He wasn't the least bit handy at those kinds of things.

One of the craziest things they did was setting fires. They would go down to the canyon with some gunnysacks and matches, wet the sacks in the creek, and then set the grass on fire. They waited to see how big it would get before putting it out with the wet sacks. Most of the time they got the fires out, but one time when Darlene, Paul and Skippy were at home alone, Paul set a fire and it got out of control so the CDF was called. That put an end to that game.

Another thing they did was to make stilts. They would take a couple of two by fours, about six or so feet in length, and nail a four by four inch block of wood to each one, about two or three feet from the bottom. They would attach some kind of strap to keep their feet from slipping off, and then they would take off walking. Although it was fun, you could get hurt if you started to fall and couldn't get your feet out from under the straps in time to jump off.

Probably the most dangerous thing they did was to slide down the hill behind the house on a sheet of tin. The hill was covered with brush and that made the tin glide down really fast. If somebody fell off, they could've gotten their head cut off, or some other body part.

And they played a dangerous game of cowboys and Indians with the rubber guns that they made. They carved the guns out of a piece of wood, and then cut strips of rubber from an inner tube; they put that piece of rubber around the end of the barrel, pulled it to the back and then fastened it behind the handle.

They made the guns big enough so the rubber would stretch as far as it could. When they took their thumb and released the rubber from the handle, it would go flying at a fast speed. When that rubber hit, it would sting like hell and leave a big welt. It could have put an eye out real easy or even killed you if it hit in the right spot. Of course, their mother forbade it, but they would go off somewhere on the mountain where she couldn't see them. The guns were so much fun, it was worth risking one's life.

But they did play some games that were not dangerous — normal games that all kids play — hide and seek, kick the can, redline, redlight-greenlight and red rover. They made up games, too, using their imaginations.

In the evenings, the kids would settle down and the family would gather around an old Victor radio. Ephriam would take the battery out of the truck and hook it up to the radio. This was a big deal, especially for the kids.

They would listen to the *Lone Ranger*, and a mystery called *Doc, Reggie and Jack*. Ephriam's favorite was *Amos and Andy*, and Mary's favorite was a soap opera that came from Rosarita Beach. That station gave listeners a free rosebush if they sent in their names. Mary did, and received her bush and planted it in the front yard. She would fertilize it with the manure from her chickens. She did get a few roses, but not many.

On December 9, 1935, **Franklin Delano (Skippy)** was born in the tent by the creek, with Dr. Benno Reinard from the CCC Camp in attendance.

Shortly after Ephriam's brother Seaton had moved up, he moved his mother, Fairzina, into the old tollhouse. Harrison moved there with her; he had always stayed with her after his father died.

Fairizina was awfully grouchy, especially when she got older. Teddy would cut wood for her; nobody else would. But as soon as he finished, she would say, "Hurry up, go on and get out of here." There was never a thank you. Fairzina stayed in the tollhouse for a while, then was moved some place near her daughter Lillie.

Bobby and Teddy sometimes stayed at the tollhouse after Fairzina was gone. The little kids would come by in the mornings on their way to school and Teddy would make cocoa for them. It was kind of spooky staying there at night after all the stories they had heard about ghosts.

112

But they kept their dog Shep there with them for protection, and kept an ax hidden under the bed.

A Spooky Trek

When Teddy was fifteen, and Pat was thirteen, their mother said she was out of supplies, and wanted them to go to Edith's house in Lodoga, which was a good two-day trip, to get some things for her. Their father and older brothers had gone off somewhere to sell wood, or to trap, and they would stay gone a few days while doing that.

The boys started out kind of late that day, as usual, and when they got to Kowalski's place — which was about three miles from their place, and the last place you hit before Brim grade — old man Kowalski told them to go on back home, that it was getting too late. But they knew they had to go on.

Mr. Kowalski gave them a sandwich and something to drink that didn't taste right, but they drank it anyway.

They started out again and by the time they got across the bridge, it was dark. There was a full moon, which cast eerie shadows around everything. They walked along, keeping their eyes and ears open for animals and things, as they always did, when Pat stopped abruptly.

"Hey, Teddy, look at that big rock," he whispered, pointing to the side of the hill. "It's moving!"

Teddy whispered back, "Pat, that ain't no rock, that's a cougar. Just keep walking, and don't make any sudden moves."

They moved slowly until they were past the cougar, and then walked briskly once again. They got partway past the mountain when Pat said, "Did you hear something?"

Teddy said, "No, Pat ... and quit trying to spook me. But, it might be an animal, or it could be a murderer coming up here to kill people."

Their mother had always warned them about people. She said there were bad people that wanted to hurt people or to kidnap kids. They were a little big to kidnap, so whoever it was would probably just want to murder them.

The noise got louder, so they hurried to the side of the road and hid behind the trees. They saw something coming up the road; when it got closer, they saw that it was a horse with a rider, but they couldn't make out who the rider was.

Someone had a barn that wasn't too far away, and Teddy said to Pat, "Let's get over to that barn, and we'll sleep there tonight instead of along this road."

They were going to stay hidden until the rider passed, but when he got close, Pat yelled out, "It's Bud!"

They were, of course, much relieved to see that it was their brother Bud, who had been away in the army. He had borrowed the horse from a man down the grade. He gave them both a ride back home and the next day he took them to get the supplies. Everybody, especially Mary, was glad to see him. He was the kind of guy that everyone liked to be around.

A Stinking Ride

One day, **Bobby, Pat** and **Teddy** took off to Lodoga to see Edith, but when they got there, she wasn't home, so they started walking on to the valley.

They had not gone very far when an old Model A pulled up and a guy that looked like some kind of a scrounge gave them a ride. The man was dirty and the car was filled with old dirty clothes and stuff.

He asked them if they wanted to work; he said that he needed some help with his goats, and could use all three of them. He knew they lived in the mountains; they had talked to him about that before, and knew they were always looking for work.

That was one stinky, miserable ride, and Teddy said he almost passed out from holding his breath to keep from breathing the bad air.

When they got to Williams, the man stopped to gas up.

Teddy got out of the car. "I'm going to hitchhike back home."

Bobby said, "I'm going to go help him with the goats, he really needs us."

Pat said, "I'm gonna stay with Bobby."

Teddy caught a ride back to Barkersville. When he got home, his mother asked, "Where are Pat and Bobby? Did they stay at Edith's?"

"No, Edith wasn't home; we met up with this guy and he said he needed help with some goats, so they went with him.

Mary got a worried look on her face and she went outside every once in a while to stare off into space. It was dark, and she was hoping that she would see the lights of a car coming up the road, bringing them home. She was worried because she told the boys never to get take rides with people they didn't know really well. She hated it when they hitchhiked.

She told them they could always get rides with Uncle Seaton, and they did sometimes, but most of the time they just took off walking. But they would go out to work all the time, and they always returned home, but that didn't stop Mary from worrying while they were gone.

They used to hunt skunks and sell the furs down in Sacramento. After selling the hides, they would look forward to having stew at the Chinaman's restaurant, for 10 cents a bowl.

Later on, they learned that their brother Earl used to sell skunk carcasses to the Chinaman, and when you had stew, it wouldn't really have rabbit in it; it was usually cat or skunk. In those days, there were no restrictions on what they could feed people.

Rides

Seaton had a model T, it was a 1923 or '24, and he kept it covered with a canvas. Teddy wanted that car in the worst way. One day he was over there and couldn't help but peek under the canvas, as he did every chance he got. Jeanette, his cousin, told him to leave it alone, that her dad didn't want kids fooling with it.

Then Teddy heard a voice coming from behind him, "Teddy, would you like to get in and sit in it?" It was his Uncle Seaton's voice. He had a calm voice, not like Teddy's father, whose voice would vibrate you when he yelled.

Teddy's ear-to-ear grin answered that question.

"Go ahead. Take the canvas off and get in." After Teddy did that, Uncle Seaton said, "How would you like to have this car?"

Teddy didn't know what was coming next, so he tried not to sound too excited when he answered, "Oh yes, I would love to have it."

"Would you be willing to cut me some wood for it?"

"I sure will, just tell me how much."

"Oh, I think a couple of cords will do," Uncle Seaton said.

Teddy started cutting right away, and it was hard to do because he didn't have much of a saw. But, he got it done, and his Uncle gave him the car. It had been setting for many years and just didn't want to run. It was a good thing that Bobby liked to work on cars; he was a good mechanic and he got the thing running. Once it was running, it needed some gas, so Bobby siphoned some out of their father's truck. They were not supposed to do that, and man did they get in trouble.

Anyhow, they figured they could go places now and one day they took off to the valley. They only got to Uncle Seaton's before running out of gas again. They had put in at least two or three gallons; that thing must have gotten about one mile to the gallon.

Occasionally, they would get gas and run it, but not very far and not very often. They ended up pushing it most of the time. It was a sorry-ass car, but it was cute. It had a rumble seat that could be removed, and a box was put in so they could run traps in it. This was only done a few times, when they were able to get gas from somewhere, or when Earl came up and they would get gas from his car.

Teddy would never siphon the gas himself; he never quite got the hang of it. But Bobby and Pat were good at it; they were ready to siphon anytime, anywhere. That's the only way they ever got gas, and so they didn't do a lot of traveling. Teddy ended up hating that car, and eventually it was abandoned at the bottom of the hill. The boys then turned their attention to an old wagon that was like the one on *Gunsmoke*. They didn't have a horse, so they just pulled it around themselves.

One time, Pat, Bobby, Teddy, and Roy and Alafair Saylor, pulled that wagon down to where the haunted house was. They were too tired to pull any more, so they left it there.

When they got home, they asked their father if he would take them back to get the wagon. He wouldn't; he said to just leave it there.

The old wagon remained at the haunted house, where it looked right at home. At times, Teddy would try to get somebody to help him go get it but nobody would. Every once in a while, he and his brothers would go down to the haunted house and fool around with the wagon, but they made sure to hightail it away from there before darkness fell.

A House Divided

Ted and May Williams had a place up there, and they fought all the time. Ted was a heavy drinker, and they had some bad fights. He didn't do much, just read pulp fiction and got drunk. May got tired of it all, kicked him out and told him she was going to get a divorce.

One day, Ephriam was driving by and saw Ted doing something to his house. Curious, he stopped. He got out, leaving Teddy, Cam and Pat in the car.

"What in the hell are you doing, Ted?" Ephriam asked, scratching his head.

"Ephriam, I'm sawing it in half, so she can have her half and I can have mine. Then I'm going to take mine and get the hell out of here."

"Are you crazy? You can't take half the house, and you're just going to have to put it back together again," Ephriam said.

"No, I won't. She wants me out, and I figure I should get half of everything."

"You're too drunk to know what you're doing; you better go sober up before you destroy your house." Ephriam shook his head in disbelief.

Ephriam left with him still sawing away at the house. He did a lot of damage to the house, but before he could completely saw it in half, his wife took a shotgun and threatened to shoot if he didn't stop. She convinced him to stop and to leave, and he was killed on the railway about three months later.

After Ted left, Teddy went over and took care of May's garden for that summer. Shortly after, she met a guy named Whitney. He was a nice guy, who always wore bib-overalls. He ran a dude ranch out of Lakeport and had a '34 Plymouth that was just like brand new.

The next summer, May and Whitney moved to a dude ranch, and wanted Teddy to go stay with them, so he did, and they really treated him well. He had a horse and would go out with the guys when they rode around the ranch. Sometimes May would take him shopping with her and they would ride around town, then come back and ride around the one- thousand-acre ranch. The ranch bordered a nudist colony, and that was such a curiosity to Teddy. He couldn't imagine letting another person see him naked, especially a female. He stayed for the summer then went back to Barkersville.

One day, out of the blue, Ephriam announced, "Kids, we're moving to town; no more walking to school."

They had moved from the homestead before, but usually it would be just for a few months, then they would come back again.

That time they moved to Kelseyville. It was a nice town and they lived by a family that had twins, Mildred and Margaret. They had a sister, Kelsey, who Johnny went with.

All of the kids had a good time while they lived there, but before long, they moved to Sites, in Colusa County.

LAKE'S LARGEST FAMILY MOVES TO COLUSA COUNTY

Lake county's largest family has moved to Colusa county and some of the other large families of Lake county will not be so overwhelmingly outclassed in competition for first honors in the future. The large family in mention is the E. B. Barkers with 15 children. A recent news item from Sites, Colusa county, states:

"Although the smallest community in Colusa county, Sites boasts the largest single family in the county and perhaps in superior California.

"It is the family of Mr. and Mrs. Ephriam Buck Barker, who moved here about a month ago from Lake county, where several of the children were born. There are fifteen children in the family, ranging in ages from 16 to 2 years—the youngest being named Franklin Delano.

"'We didn't run out of names,' Mrs. Barker explained, 'but we liked Franklin Delano as a name, and we like the man, too.'

"'Yes, we find trouble getting a house with enough rooms to conveniently place our flock of boys and girls,' Barker commented, 'but we try to get the largest house available and make the best of the situation.' Every member of the family excepting one, Edythe Barker, lives at home. Edythe is employed in College City.

"Several of the older boys are engaged with their father in clearing lands and chopping wood on the Herman Dunlap, Jr., holdings.

"The children of age attend the Antelope valley district school near Sites and of which Mrs. Clara Gerber is teacher. All of them are apt and bright.

"The Barkers consider themselves specially fortunate that every member of their brood is in good health

The Rubber Room

While living in Sites, Johnny, Bobby, Pat and Teddy left for Colusa one morning to see about getting work. They were in an old Buick they had borrowed from a family friend. They broke down on a back road outside of Colusa. It was nighttime, so they had to sleep in the car and wait for daylight so Bobby could try and fix it.

They had been sleeping for a while when Teddy was awakened by red lights flashing all around them. "Oh my God, it's the posse!" he yelled out. That jolted the others awake.

Two officers, one fat, and one really skinny, came up to the boy's car and shined a flashlight on them.

"Get out of the cars, boys," one of the officers said as he opened the driver's door. The boys piled out, and one of the officers searched the car, while the other one questioned the boys.

"What are you guys doing out here this time of night?" the fat officer asked as he shined the light in each boy's face.

Johnny answered, "We came here to look for work, and our car broke down here."

The other officer came over to them and said, "We gotta take you in; we have some questions that need to be answered."

They piled the boys in the back seat of the squad car and took them to Colusa county jail.

When they got inside the jail, the fat officer, grinning, said, "It's your lucky night boys; all the cells are full, we're gonna have to put you in the rubber room."

"What's that?" Johnny and Pat asked simultaneously.

The fat officer, still grinning, answered, "Just what I said; it's a room covered with rubber. Don't worry, you're gonna have fun in there. You can take turns bouncing each other's head against the wall."

"Why would you need a room like that?" Johnny asked.

"For the crazies. They can bang their heads against the walls or the floor without knocking their brains out," the grinning officer said.

"You can't keep us here. We haven't committed any crimes," Johnny said emphatically.

"Is that right? Well, you just hide and watch, fresh mouth," the obnoxious officer said.

"Why did you bring us here? What were you gonna ask us questions about?" Pat asked.

"Never mind about that," said Officer String Bean, who had sat down at the desk, and put his feet up. "We're gonna do that in the morning."

The boys were rounded up and put in the rubber room, and at least they had a warm place to sleep. In the morning, they were told that a rancher had complained that a bunch of kids had been sleeping on his property. They let the boys go without questioning them, and they didn't even feed them or take them back to the car. They had to walk for hours to get to the car. Bobby got it going, and they continued on their way, all wishing they had stayed at home.

Shortly after that, the family went to a hop camp, and that's where Teddy met Alice Martha Grant, the prettiest girl that he had ever laid eyes on. He fell hard the first time he looked at her and knew that she was the one for him.

His Uncle Seaton had told him that when you fall in love for real, you would know it. He also told him that a woman could destroy you or make you the happiest man in the world. His uncle spoke from experience, as he had been married twice.

Teddy was a Casanova; the girls always did like him, even older women. It could've been his hair; it was black and wavy just like Robert Taylor's. Anyway, Alice bothered him so much that he knew he would have to marry her.

They promised to write to each other, but after Teddy left there, he knew he couldn't be away from her too long so he went to Fort Bragg, where she lived, and went to work for a crazy redheaded lady. She had a dairy and was so lazy, she never did a thing; Teddy had to do the whole damned shabutal. But she had a '35 Ford Coupe that he got to run around in. It was very seldom taken out of the garage, so it was still like new. She also had a milk truck that he would drive her teenage twins around in, delivering milk.

Teddy stayed at the dairy for about a year before going to work at a lumber mill as a choke setter. He got paid $50 a month at the dairy and got paid by the hour at the mill. He worked there long enough to buy a house, and a Ford that had a factory default for $500. It would burn a gallon of oil every ten miles, but it did get him and Alice to Reno, Nevada, where they were married on Oct. 20, 1942.

Rich Little Poor Girl

I was born on April 28, 1938, near Upper Lake, California, in a cabin that was one of a complex of cabins used as a motel. I was the eighteenth child. Mama named me **Ada Florence**, after Uncle Cam's wife.

Papa was with Mama most of the time during labor, which he said was long and very painful. I was delivered by Dr. M. C. Beil, and Papa told me I was a difficult breech birth.

Papa and Mama had come down from Barkersville the day before, and Papa had rented two cabins, anticipating the birth. He had rented two because he needed a room for the six children they brought with them—Darlene, Paul, Gloria, Jimmie, Jackie and Skippy.

Darlene, who wasn't quite eight, was the oldest of the children and was in charge when Papa wasn't there. She was told she was to go to the cabin next door where Mama was, only if necessary. Papa checked on the kids often, as they would get quite noisy and he would have to go quiet them. Darlene was a skinny little thing, but she was tough and managed to keep things under control until the boys started jumping up and down on the floor. They jumped so hard that they broke the floorboards. She went to tell Papa, and when she got to the door, Papa told her to come inside. The doctor, who was just about to leave, ordered Mama to stay in bed for a few days.

When Darlene saw the bundle in Mama's arms, she grinned and went to the bed.

Mama motioned her to sit down beside her, and then handed the

bundle to Darlene and said, "Here's your baby girl."

Before I was born, Darlene had told Mama that she was going to take care of the new baby and that she hoped it would be a girl.

I let out a cry about then, and Mama asked, "Do you still want to take care of her?"

Darlene said, "Yes, I do, and I won't let any one else touch her." She meant it.

And she did take care of me. She bathed me, fed me, and protected me from harm as best she could. And she was there standing up for me against anyone. Our brothers were afraid to give Darlene a bad time, because she could take care of herself and wouldn't hesitate to do bodily harm if need be. She was my hero.

After my birth, the family returned to Barkersville where Papa and

the boys continued cutting wood and knocking poles to sell to the prune farmers. All the kids who were old enough had to peel those poles. Not fun!

On December 30, 1940, **Charles Lewis** was born in Lakeport, California, and **Susan Jane** was born April 12, 1942 in Lakeport.

My earliest memory was when our house caught on fire when Susie was about

two-weeks-old, and I had just turned four. We were taken to a neighbors' house, and the lady of the house was always getting after me because I wouldn't keep my hands off the new baby. I thought she was rude and I told her: "This is not your baby, it's mine. "

My earliest memory of the homestead was when I was around five. For my fifth birthday, Mama made a big cake with pink frosting and made a little one just like it for me to have for myself. I took the little cake to the middle of the hill, sat amongst the golden poppies and bluebells and slowly ate it, savoring every bite. I was in heaven as I sat there alone enjoying my cake and listening to the birds singing. The other kids were busy eating the big cake, so I was really enjoying my time alone. There wasn't a gift for me, and that's why Mama made the little cake; it was my gift and I appreciated it so much.

First Doll

I used my imagination to be whatever, whoever or wherever I wanted, and it worked very well for me. The only thing that I can remember aching to have was a doll, but I made do with what I could find to take the place of a baby doll. My doll was a two by four piece of wood about one foot long. I drew eyes, a nose, and a mouth on it and put a nail at the top so I could walk it. I kept it with me night and day.

It satisfied my maternal instincts until one day Papa brought a doll for Gloria. I was crushed; I wanted it so badly, and I knew that Gloria didn't like babies the way I did. She wouldn't let me touch that doll. She was an ornery one, that girl. The reason Papa gave it to her, I guess, was because she was the oldest, but I thought it was because he liked her better. He told everyone that she was his baby, because she was the only one of his kids that he delivered by himself.

I finally got my own beautiful baby doll when Mama's sister Madge came to visit and brought two dolls—one for Susie and one for me. I adored that doll. It had a composition head, arms and legs, but the body was cloth, making it nice to cuddle. I don't think I put her down for a week.

She came to a sad end though at the hands of my little brother Charlie. There was a small table in the living room that I would set my doll on when I fed her, and sometimes I would leave her sitting there while I went off to do something else. One day Charlie knocked her off, breaking her head. I was devastated. It was glued back together several times, but the glue never held.

I don't remember getting another doll when I was a little girl, but I did come to own quite a few after I grew up. I am especially fond of Schoenhut dolls, and I think it's because they're wooden. It reminds me of my handmade doll.

Susie & Ada

Someone wanted to buy my sister Susie when she was a baby. She was beautiful, with her light hair and big green eyes, and sometimes when I was fighting with her, I wondered why Mama hadn't sold her. I always had to give in to her.

I wanted a bed for my doll and asked Mama if I could have the next cardboard box she got. She said the next time she got one big enough she would give it to me. Well, when she got the box, Susie started crying and said that she wanted it for her doll, and of course, she got it.

But I really did love my little sister, and one time when she was about two, she choked on a fish bone, and I really got frightened. Mama told us to never give her a bite of fish, but someone did, not checking it for bones.

Mama panicked as she laid Susie over her knee and slapped her on the back. Finally, Susie coughed up the bone, and we were all so happy about that.

Spring and summer: a Joyous Time

In the spring, the mountainside that our house sat on was covered with golden poppies and bluebells. What a beautiful sight that was. I loved springtime, with the flowers in bloom and the birds and animals having their babies; it was a joyous time for me. The baby cottontail rabbits were the cutest things, and the baby quail were so adorable, following their mama all around. And the baby chicks from the chickens Mama kept were so sweet.

I would watch the bald eagles soar overhead on their way to the top of the mountain where they made their nests on the rocks. My brothers told me that the eagles had little houses up there in which they had little furnishings. I had the most fabulous picture in my mind about those little houses and wanted to go there so badly.

The summers at the homestead were ideal. We had the greatest swimming hole at the creek, and in spring and summer, it was our haven. We spent all day there swimming, catching tadpoles, and watching water snakes and water dogs swimming about. And that smell was the most pleasant that I had ever experienced. It was so pleasant lying under a tree on the creek bank with the coolness of the dirt under you, daydreaming about all the good things that could happen. If there were better places to be in the world, you couldn't have convinced me.

On one of those beautiful summer days, Mama was going to the creek to wash clothes. I ran ahead, eager to get to the big rock so I jump into the cool water. As I neared the rock, I saw something lying on it. . When I got to it, I found it was a blue bathing suit with little white stars all over it.

I was the happiest kid on earth that day because I had wanted a swimming suit so badly and had asked Mama if I could have one.

The suit fit perfectly, and my summer was made that day. Someone who had gone swimming there had just forgotten it, but Mama said that maybe I had wished so hard that it came true. I was convinced.

Another summer day when I was out catching tadpoles at the creek, I was so involved in my task that I didn't see the other kids leave. I don't know how long it was before I noticed they were gone, but when I did, I glanced around to see if they were nearby. I didn't see them, but what I did see scared the heck out of me. I saw a huge turtle, not too far from me, walking off into the woods. It looked big enough for me to ride on. It must have been two feet long.

I took off running as my fast as my little legs could carry me, and running was one thing I could do very well. I got home and told Mama what I had seen.

"Ada Florence, you have such an imagination!"

"It's true, Mama. It was really that big," I said.

I tried to convince my brothers to go find it, but they just laughed at me. Jimmie said that the sun had warped my brain.

I know what I saw wasn't my imagination, and for quite a while after that, I watched for those turtles. I also thought that if turtles got that big, so could other varmints, like lizards or snakes.

The creek bed was the greatest place; kids could do a lot of things there. Tree limbs that had been broken off by the floods lay all over and they made great horses. Darlene had the best one; it was tall and white and it was named Silver.

We all had our own horse and no one was supposed to ride someone else's, but we couldn't resist getting on Darlene's. Once, one of the boys made that mistake and ended up with a good-sized cut on his head from being knocked off and landing headfirst on the rocks below.

When we weren't playing in the creek, Darlene and I would play house down under a huge tree by the creek. The tree had vines that hung down to the ground completely enclosing the area underneath it. It was fun swinging on those vines, too. We made mud pies and cakes and set them on the rocks to dry. Sometimes the boys would destroy them and say that the dogs did it, but we knew better.

One day we hid and watched them start to do their dirty deed. Boy, they were surprised when Darlene let out a yell and took off after them with a huge tree branch. They scattered like cockroaches.

I don't remember playing any games with Gloria when we were kids. She didn't like to do much with me. She was always grouchy to me.

But Gloria was nice to me on one occasion; that was the time she wanted to stay all night with a girl that lived down by the creek and Mama said she could, but only if she took me.

I didn't want to go; I had never stayed away from the family all night. But I went, for her sake. We got to the girl's house and played for a while, but when it was almost dark, Gloria decided she wanted to go home. I didn't mind going home, but I did mind walking all that way in the dark.

We took off running and made sure we didn't pass under any trees, because we didn't want the hootie paddies to jump on us. Those creatures live in the trees, and if you walk under their trees when it's dark, they'll attack you.

When we grew up, Gloria and I did become close, and we spent a lot of time together.

Living up in those mountains, Mama cautioned us about strangers that came up there. She told us never to go near their cars, and if we were near the road, we would hide whenever we saw a car coming. This made me overly aware of all dangers that can beset someone, but I am sure genetics had something to do with it because Mama was the same way.

Hoboes came up to our house sometimes; Mama fixed them food and they would eat on the porch. We weren't afraid of them; I guess because we knew they couldn't kidnap us. But Mama would tell us to go inside, and she kept an eye on them until she saw them disappear from view as they walked away.

They came off the trains that ran on the nearby tracks, and I envied them. I loved to hear the whistle blowing in the distance and wanted so much to get on that train so it could carry me to one of the far away places that I yearned to see. I always wanted to hop a freight train, and I still have the urge to do that.

Gloria--Pat--Darlene

School Days

In 1944, we lived in Maxwell, California, and I started first grade. At least, I was supposed to start, but after Darlene got me to the office and tried to leave me alone with the principal, I changed my mind and told her I wanted to go home.

But the principal said, "You'll be just fine, Ada. I'll be taking you to your class."

I didn't like the guy's looks. His eyes were beady, and he reminded me of the picture of the wolf in my Little Red Riding Hood storybook. I didn't trust his wolfish smile either.

"See you later." Darlene opened the door to leave.

"I want to go home," I yelled out to her. I was terrified.

"She'll be just fine here. Go on to your class, Darlene."

He tried being nice. "Would you like some Milk?"

I shook my head. "I want to go home."

"You can't right now. You have to go to class."

"I'm going to find Darlene."

He shook his head no. The bell rang. He took me to my classroom, and the teacher showed me to my desk.

I wouldn't sit down. "I want to go home."

The teacher sent for Darlene.

"**Ada,** you have to sit down. That's what you do in school." Darlene got a little chair, put it beside mine, and stayed with me for a while.

But as soon as she left, I got up and told the teacher I wanted to go home.

The teacher had a student take me back to the principal.

The principal swatted me on the behind. "You have to go back to class," he said.

Of course, that only made it worse and justified my dislike of him.

He called Darlene to his office then. "Take Ada home. She can't come back until next school year."

And that was fine by me.

The next year I started first grade in Fruto, and I loved going to that school. It was a one-room schoolhouse, and I had my brothers and sisters there with me.

While we were living in Maxwell, President Roosevelt died on April 12, 1945. It was such a sad day; Mama spent the whole day crying.

I spent most of the day sitting in a tree in our front yard, the place I went to when I was troubled. It was my sister Susie's third birthday.

The War

When World War II was going on, my brother Bud was in the army and fighting someplace that I thought had an intriguing name. Mama was so worried about him, and I knew he was in danger of being killed, but I also thought that he must have been having quite an adventure in that faraway place. He served in the army from 1941 to 1946.

When he came home, I can only remember one story that he told about the war, and it horrified me. He said that soldiers were told to shoot women who were riding bicycles because they might be carrying hand grenades. He said some of the women would even have babies with them. I didn't ask if he ever shot one of them; I didn't want to know.

Soon after **Bud** was discharged from the army, he took us to see a movie about the war. There were Japanese soldiers in it, and when we got home, he fixed us a dinner of stew, and I couldn't eat it—I identified the taste with those soldiers and it made me sick.

I remember the ration books that we had for certain foods. The one I worried most about was the one for sugar. If we couldn't get enough sugar, it would be the worst thing that ever happened to me in my five years of life, as it could put an end to all the good things that made life worth living: things like the cakes, cookies and cinnamon rolls that Mama made when she did her bread making. Although her light bread was heavenly, I preferred the sweet stuff. She also made candy out of orange peelings and I dearly loved that because it was extra sweet.

Mama was such a good cook and could make any food taste great. We had a lot of venison; it is the best meat I have ever tasted. We would have it fried or roasted. We ate lots of jackrabbits and they were good. Someone gave us some domestic rabbits, and although Mama cooked them the same way as she did the jackrabbits, no one liked them.

Food was scarce so we learned to appreciate any food that we got. But I just couldn't appreciate the artichokes that my sister-in-law Doris tried to make us eat. To me they were not food; you couldn't even eat the whole thing, you had to scrape off little bits from the petals and that wasn't worth doing. She got complaints from all of us kids.

For breakfast, we had pancakes and oatmeal most of the time, but sometimes, we would have fried potatoes, eggs and salt pork. We also had hot Ralston, and Mama's favorite thing to have with her coffee was Nabisco Shredded Wheat Biscuits with butter.

Another pleasant memory is of the big wood range. I loved the aroma that came from it when Mama cooked or baked. I loved the smell of the wood burning and the feel of warmth on those cold mornings. And it provided a sanctuary when I wasn't feeling well. There was a space between the stove and the wall where I would take my blanket and lie down. It made a perfect place to convalesce. To this day, I still a have passion for those big wood ranges.

There was an apple orchard at the Abel's place, and as soon as the trees had little green apples, we wanted to pick some. But I can't remember if we did that, because Mama told us not to go there; she didn't want us to eat green apples. We kids would say that she thought they would give us carlic-marbles, whatever the heck that was.

Papa once brought home cases of the syrup that they used in the soda fountains to make Pepsi-Cola. Oh, boy, did I love that sweet taste! We would put the bottles in the spring to cool, since we had no icebox, and that worked just fine, because the water in our spring was always very cold.

The fact that we didn't have an icebox, electricity or inside plumbing, wasn't a hardship for us kids. The kerosene lamps put out enough light for whatever we did in the evenings, and the only time the outhouse was a problem was when somebody had the runs or there was no toilet paper. But we did have substitutes for the paper because we always had magazines or catalogs.

A Skunk in the Kitchen

Mama would always rise before daybreak. Her footsteps in the kitchen would wake me, and I wanted to jump out of bed as soon as I heard her building the fire in her big wood range. But I didn't, because Mama wanted to have some time alone before anyone else got up.

I have always been a morning person. To me it's the best part of the day, and there's an excitement in the beginning of each new day, like something wonderful and exciting just has to happen.

I would lie there listening to the fire crackle and smell the coffee brewing. I loved that smell; I loved the taste, too, and I drank coffee any chance I got. Many times, when I got up before any of the other kids, Mama would let me have coffee with her. It was one of my most pleasant memories.

Mama sang in the mornings. She would sing "Rock of Ages," "Tramp on the Street," "Buckle Down Buck Private" and other religious songs.

However, she wasn't singing one morning. Instead, she was yelling, "Ephriam, get up and get this skunk out of the kitchen!"

I cringed and stuck my head under the covers. I was sleeping in a bed with Darlene and Gloria, and I was in the middle. Those girls decided they would have some fun and tease me.

"It's gonna come in here, Ada, and you're the one it's gonna get." **Gloria** yanked the covers from over my head.

"You're lying." I pulled the covers back over my head.

"It's true. They only get the one that sleeps in the middle of the bed," Darlene, my hero, said.

It didn't make sense to me, but I knew Darlene was an honest person, so I stayed as still as I could under the covers, just in case.

Papa managed to chase the skunk out without it spraying the house or him.

After that incident, I never felt the same about sleeping in the middle again. I would stay awake for hours worrying that a skunk might get me.

Childhood Daydreams

Whenever Papa made a trip to the dump, he brought home bundles of magazines like *The Saturday Evening Post*, *Look*, and *Life* that had been tied together with string. People did this so others could take them. I devoured those magazines, and before I could read, I would pester anyone around to read the stories to me. Sometimes my older brothers would do this, but usually it was Mama or Darlene.

The movie stars and anybody that was in the music business fascinated me. And I was interested in the stories about the war and anything to do with politics. I wanted to know about the different countries. I had an intense need to know about almost everything.

We covered the walls of the house with pictures from the magazines, and I really liked that; I pretended they were our company and made them tea and had conversations with them.

I daydreamed about one day being a great dancer and singer and, of course, I would be beautiful like Hedy Lamarr. When I was about eight, someone showed me a picture of Elizabeth Taylor in a magazine and told me that I resembled her—that I had the same coloring with dark hair, blue eyes, and freckles. Although I would have preferred a comment on resembling Hedy, I was more certain than ever that I was destined to be a great star.

But there was one person that told me there was no way that I could ever be a dancer or singer or go to Hollywood—my oldest sister

Edith. She would say the cruelest things to me.

She had married before I was born, so I never lived with her, and maybe that's why she didn't seem like a sister. Her first child, a girl, was born one week after I was. Shirley was a beautiful child with dark curly hair and a little round face. She was named after Shirley Temple, and Edith told me that Shirley would be the one that would be going to Hollywood. She said my legs were too skinny and that Shirley had a better singing voice. I didn't believe that about the singing because I had heard Shirley sing, and it wasn't that great, but the legs comment I believed because my skinny little legs paled in comparison to Shirley's chubby ones.

The worst thing she did happened when I was six. We were in a  hop camp in Ukiah, and she was going to take her children and her siblings—Charlie, Susie and me—to the carnival. When it was time to go, she decided that I couldn't go because I had a stain on my dress. I had never been to a carnival before, and although it took a lot to make me cry, I sobbed my heart out.

But **Edith** could be nice sometimes, and I was so happy when she was; I kept wishing that she would stop being so cruel not only to me but to others too.

I was happy when Edith and her family came to visit, though; I loved to play with Shirley and her sister Mary. It was a real treat for me to have girls my age to play with, and I was sad when they left.

On one of the trips that Edith made to Barkersville, she arrived in the middle of the night, in a car that had a rumble seat. When I found out that Shirley got to ride in that seat all the way up the mountain, I was so envious. I thought that had to be the grandest thing to do.

Brothers

At the homestead, we had to go to the spring and get water every day, and one day Mama sent Jackie and Jimmie for water, and gave me my little bucket and said I was to go with them. As we drew near the spring, we saw a porcupine there trying to get a drink. It looked so big and menacing.

I tried to relate to my fears to my brothers. "He's gonna attack us. I'm going back home."

Jimmie shushed me. "Be quiet or he'll throw his quills at us."

We stood motionless until it sauntered off, and then we proceeded to get the water. Those "gentlemen" brothers of mine filled their buckets, and before I had a chance to fill mine, they took off like a bat-out-of-hell, leaving me behind to face that porcupine, which I was sure was just waiting to come out and get me. I wasn't about to take any chances of that happening, so I threw down my bucket and took off after them.

When I got to the house, Mama asked me, "Where's your bucket of water?"

"I couldn't fill my bucket. Jackie and Jimmie left me there alone with that porcupine, and I was afraid it would get me."

"She's lying. She just didn't want to get any water. You know how stubborn she is," the lying Jimmie said.

"He's the one that's lying, Mama; just ask Jackie," I said desperately.

"Jackie, I ain't lying, am I?" Jimmie said really fast.

Jackie shook his head in agreement with Jimmie.

I don't know why Mama believed them instead of me, but apparently, she did, because she made me go back to the spring by myself to get my bucket of water, which I did keeping an eye out for that old porcupine.

When I was seven years old, I wanted a bike so badly, but there was only one bike around and it belonged to Jimmie. I wanted to ride it, but Jimmie had given me orders not to touch it, and Mama told me to stay off it. However, I couldn't resist, and I was willing to risk a brother's wrath and a broken neck.

I got home earlier than the other kids and as soon as I did, I headed straight for the bike. I tried to get on it and away from the house before Mama could stop me.

It was huge, well, to me anyway, and I had to stand on the porch to get on it. It took me a while to do that, but once I got going, I took off down the road. Although I always ended up taking a fall before getting too far and ended up with bruises and scrapes from head to toe, I did learn to ride.

Another thing that my brothers didn't want me to touch were their  comic books. But occasionally I would get my own, and I chose the horror comics. I liked "The Vault of Horrors," "Witches Caldron," and "Tales from the Crypt."

The younger boys loved to tease me, **Jimmie** more than the others. He got such a kick out of it.

He was the funniest kid; we laughed at him so much, and he was a lot of fun--except when he was teasing me.

But I've forgiven for that, and now I enjoy his company more than ever.

Jackie sometimes joined in with the teasing, but he wasn't as bad as Jimmie. He was quite a witty guy--still is. We've got a lot of witty people in our family, but Jackie is right there at the top.

Skippy didn't tease me very much. He was always good to me. He was so handsome, and the girls in school would tell me how cute he was and ask questions about him. Skippy was a quiet, softhearted guy and was ready to help anyone who was in need. He had passionate feelings about things and that led him into a bad marriage that may, in part, have led to his death. Skippy was killed June 15, 1979, when his jeep rolled over a cliff. He was forty-four years old.

Two days before his death, I had one of my prophetic dreams. I dreamed I was at Darlene's house. We were sitting at her table, and she told me that her husband Bill had died. I was devastated and couldn't figure out why. I wasn't fond of her husband and wouldn't have been that upset finding out about his death. Another thing that was weird was that Darlene wasn't as upset as I was. In the dream, I kept trying to figure out why I was so upset, and why I couldn't stop wailing from the pain I was feeling.

When I woke up, I had that horrible feeling of dread that I get with these kinds of dreams, and I waited for the bad news that would come—and it did come—two days later by a phone call from my sister Susie, telling me that Skippy had been killed. I was stunned, and I was feeling the same terrible pain that I had felt in my dream.

Jimmie—Skippy—Jackie

It took me a long time to come to terms with Skippy's death, and exactly one year to the day of his death, I had a dream that he was sitting at a table with Gloria and me, and we were talking and laughing and having so much fun—then he got up and told us he had to leave.

I couldn't lose him again, so I said, "Skippy, I'm going with you."

"No, Ada, you can't come with me this time," he said.

I started to cry, and he said, "Ada, I'll be back to see you guys every now and then. Don't feel bad, it'll be okay."

He walked out and the next thing I knew, he was walking on a highway that was going up a mountain, and I was walking behind him, trying to catch up.

"Skippy, wait for me!" I called.

He turned around and said, "Go back, Ada. You can't come with me this time. Please go back." And then he turned and started walking up the hill again.

I wanted to follow but I couldn't get my legs to move, so I just stood there and watched him walk out of sight. Then I woke up.

The Boys with Papa

All my brothers were good-looking. Bobby was so gorgeous; he had black hair, beautiful eyes and the greatest smile. When he was three, somebody that was called "The Artichoke King" in the Salinas valley, wanted to buy him for fifty thousand dollars.

I adored Bobby; he treated me like a princess. He would always greet me with "hello, beautiful." He would treat all the little kids special. He would take us for walks, sing songs to us, and always had that beautiful smile ready for us. But Bobby had a sad side to him, and he would get the saddest look in his eyes sometimes. In most of his pictures, he has that look and it hurt me to see him like that.

Once, when he was helping Papa cut wood on the buzz saw, Bobby slipped and fell into the blade, severely cutting his arm about four inches below the shoulder. He was taken to the hospital and had several stitches, but the cut healed well.

Now, Johnny, he was good-looking, but he would do that thing with his eyelids, turning them up so you could see the red underside. Man, that really freaked us out. That was so ugly. He loved to scare us kids; he was the best storyteller, and when he told us spooky stories, we believed them. I loved those stories; I loved being scared by them, and those kinds of stories, and mysteries are still my favorite.

Johnny could be so boisterous; he loved to argue (most people in our family are accused of loving to do this) and I can remember a lot of the arguing was about religion. Johnny was a nonbeliever, and once someone told him if he didn't stop saying such awful things, God might strike him dead.

He laughed, looked upwards, and spread his arms out and yelled, "Here I am, God. Strike me dead!"

I thought that he went too far that time, and that God must be so mad at him. I closed my eyes and waited to hear the thunder from the lightning bolt that was going to do him in, but all I heard was Johnny laughing even harder.

I always wished that he wouldn't talk like that because Mama didn't like it. Johnny was quite intelligent, and whenever someone would bring up a subject for discussion, he would know something about it, most times more than the person who brought it up. When Johnny wasn't drunk, I enjoyed his company.

Johnny died May 2002, from heart failure at age eighty.

I don't really remember much about my older brothers, especially Earl, Teddy, Pat, Cam, and Benny. They worked away from home a lot and joined the service at an early age.

Earl was somewhat of a stranger to me when I was growing up, and I think it was because I never lived with him. He was away from home before I was born, and after he married, I don't remember a lot of visits from him.

Ten of my brothers were in the service: Bud, Earl, Teddy, John, Cam, Benny and **Paul** were in the army. Jim, Jack and Skippy were in the marines. Bud was in World War II, and Paul was in the Korean War. Bud made it through without any wounds; Paul suffered from frostbite, which damaged some of his toes, and he was sent home.

Most of my brothers were decent people, but there were a few that had serious problems, and alcohol was the cause of a lot of them.

Pat was the one that had the worst alcohol problem. He was an odd guy; he did what he pleased regardless of how it affected anyone else. Mama said that he was born without a conscience, and the memories I have of Pat are of him always being in some kind of trouble. I remember Mama getting after him for one thing or another. He was exceptionally smart in many ways, and could inveigle others to fall for his scams, of which he had many.

A Little Boy Crippled

Some times were painful. We were living in Ukiah, California, in 1943 when Charlie, who was three, started complaining about his hip hurting. Papa thought it was because he had sat on the spare tire that was in the bed of the truck. But the pain got worse, so they took him to the doctor and found out that he had polio.

Charlie never had to be in an iron lung. It never affected his lungs, but it ended up crippling one of his legs. And I guess that was something to be thankful for, because so many other children had to have help with their breathing. There were a lot of deaths from that horrible disease. Some hospitals were filled with polio victims at that time.

We were quarantined for a while. After the quarantine was up, and we had returned to the homestead, Mama would exercise Charlie's leg, day after day, for long periods. She was so patient with him.

Periodically, he had to be taken to Sister Kinney's Hospital in San Francisco, and I remember going there with Mama on a Greyhound bus. On one of those times, some sailors at the bus station sat with us. They were very nice. They loved Susie, who was a darling baby, and they were so good to Charlie. They gave us some coins from a foreign country where they had been stationed.

Charlie was the cutest little guy and so very funny. He would make up the cutest stories to entertain us.

My parents would put their bed out on the porch in the summer and in the evenings, we would sit out there with Mama and talk for hours or until Papa got home, and he usually got home late.

Most of the time, the little ones ended up falling asleep on the bed with her.

On one of those late evenings, with an awesome, huge silver moon smiling down on us, Charlie sat for the longest time, mesmerized, staring at it.

After a while, he said, "Mama, I remember being up with Jesus before I was born."

Mama laughed and hugged him, then said, "You certainly have a good memory, Charlie. Tell us what you were doing up there with Jesus." He said, still staring at the moon, "I was just letting Jesus take care of me."

But he suffered so much as a little boy. At school one day, he watched some boys playing baseball, and he started to cry and bang his head on the wall, out of frustration from not being able to run and play with them. My heart ached and I cried with him.

Papa bought Charlie a wagon and a tricycle, and I was overjoyed. I pushed him around in the wagon, and when he didn't want to play with it, I would get to. I got to ride the tricycle as well; it was a little small for me, but I didn't care, I was just so happy to have something to ride.

I had some good times with Charlie, even though he was such a brat when he was between the ages of ten and fourteen, as most boys are.

When Charlie got older, he took a liking to alcohol and could be belligerent when he was drunk, but he was a lot of fun when he was sober.

Papa & Charlie

Mama's Sorrows

Mama not only had to contend with all the troubles of her children, she had to contend with Papa's weaknesses as well.

Some times, she would wait for him to bring food home, and he would come in late, having had too much to drink. This happened more than a few times, and when it did, I would beg Mama not to talk to him. I thought if she wouldn't talk when he tried to start an argument, he would just shut up and go to bed. Of course, it didn't work. If she didn't talk, he would get madder than ever.

I never forgave Papa for anything he said or did to hurt Mama, but as I got older, I understood somewhat of what he was going through. Those were hard times, and he could very easily have left us at any time. His drinking was the main problem. He was an alcoholic; the temptation was great, and the wine was cheap.

Besides hating alcohol, Mama also hated smoking and cussing. The boys were careful not to cuss around Mama, and their cuss words were tame compared to the ones used today. As children, if she heard us say a bad word, we would get our mouths washed out with soap.

It was easy for me as a child to understand what Mama was going through. I felt every bit of her disappointments and sadness. I stuck close to her at those times, holding her hand and saying things to comfort her; and I couldn't go to sleep at night until she and Papa had stopped talking.

And Mama suffered so much with her children, and as much as I loved Darlene, I knew that she worried Mama a lot.

Once, when Darlene was sixteen, she was about to leave with her boyfriend, Freddy, to go down to the valley. Cam was going with them. Freddy had been drinking, and Mama begged Darlene not to go, telling her they were going to have an accident. She went anyway.

A few hours after they were gone, the sheriff came up to the house and told Mama that Freddy's truck went over a bank, and that Darlene and Cam were injured. Darlene broke her foot and **Cam** had a broken back, but Freddy wasn't hurt.

Mama said she knew they were going to have an accident because she had dreamed it the night before.

Darlene caught a ride to town with the mailman when she didn't have any other way to get there. She needed her friends around at all times.

Once, when Don Schragl was her boyfriend (yes, the same Don that later married sister Edith) and he came up to see her, Pat and Cam talked him into going somewhere with them, but they didn't want

Darlene to go. The guys piled into Don's convertible, and when Darlene tried getting in, Cam pushed her back and told Don to take off. When Don goosed it, Darlene grabbed hold of the bumper, fell down, and was dragged a ways before letting go. Don floored it, leaving her in the dust, screaming at the top of her lungs.

I hated it when Darlene did things like that. I told her once that she shouldn't do things to upset Mama. She just said, "Oh, Ada Flirts, I don't want to hurt Mama, you know that, but sometimes I just have to get away from here or I would go crazy. Someday, you'll understand what I mean."

But I never did. Oh, there were times when I wanted to do things and Papa wouldn't let me, but I never went against his wishes.

Another time that was bad was when Bobby got drunk one night and had an argument with his brothers. He got a hunting knife, put it to his chest, and threatened to push it into his heart.

Papa and the boys tried to get him to put the knife down, but he wouldn't. They were afraid to grab it from him, because if they made a move toward him, he might do what he had threatened.

The boys huddled together and made a plan; Cam got on one side and Pat on the other, and they both moved at the same time, grabbed Bobby's arms and threw him to the floor. They wrestled the knife from him and took him out to the shack so he could sleep it off.

While all this was going on, Mama and us little kids stayed in the bedroom. I was so worried that Bobby was going to be hurt, and I can just imagine what Mama was going through.

Mama's Death

I hated nights when I was child and I still do. As a small child in Barkersville, when I closed my eyes to go to sleep, I would see the image of a man standing on a cliff. He would be standing there and then he would raise his arms out from his sides and would fall forward. I would panic, open my eyes, and call to Mama. This happened night after night.

Other things happened that made me dread going to bed as well. I've always had nightmares, but the prophetic dreams were the ones that really frightened me. What I must have put Mama through, calling to her at all times of the night. I don't see how she could have been so patient with me.

One of the worst dreams I ever had was when I was ten. In that dream, I was in a room that had blood clots all over the floor, and I was picking them up and putting them in a bucket. But whenever I picked one up, another would appear in its place.

I was frantic. I knew I had to get the clots in that bucket or something terrible was going to happen. I had such a feeling of helplessness in that dream. I awoke terrified and knew that the dream wasn't one of my normal nightmares. There was feeling of dread that stayed with me after that dream, and a few days later, I found out why.

Unbeknownst to me, Mama had been diagnosed with cancer of the bladder, and on a trip to the doctor, we stopped to go to the restroom. I saw the blood in the toilet after Mama had used it, and thought immediately of my dream. I had that same feeling of dread and helplessness.

That was the most terrible time in my life. I couldn't shake that feeling of doom, and I would try to play so I could forget about it, but it didn't work. I just stuck close to **Mama** all the time.

Around the first part of August in 1948, we went to Colusa where Darlene lived in some court that had a bunch of cabins. Other family members lived in the court, as well. I remember being in three of the cabins, and I remember Darlene's, but I can't remember who actually lived in the others. I do know that my brother Ted's wife, Alice, was there, and she was pregnant.

We hadn't been there long when Alice thought she was having labor pains, and Mama and Papa were going to take her to the hospital. I'll never forget what Mama said before they left, because those would be the last words I would ever hear her speak.

She called to us to come to her and then she said, "We're taking Alice to the hospital, so you kids be good. I'll be back soon." She walked toward the car, but when she got almost to it, she turned, laughed and said, "I might be the one they'll keep."

My heart fell to my stomach, and that horrible feeling of doom was even stronger than before. I knew she wouldn't be coming back. They did keep Mama, and Alice was sent home.

I wanted to go visit Mama in the hospital, and one afternoon,

Darlene told me she would take me when it was visiting hours. She washed and pressed my dress earlier that day, and when she got me ready, she told me not to go outside and play. But I couldn't resist going out to play jacks and, of course, I got dirty. When it was time to leave, she saw how dirty I was and told me that I couldn't go. I was crushed. I couldn't believe that Darlene was pulling an Edith on me, but she did, and took Susie and Charlie and left me behind.

Mama had an operation August 11, 1948, and died one week later on August 18, 1948. She was fifty years old.

There have been rumors that Mama died as a result of having the number of children she had, but that is not the case. The doctor told the family that she had been in good health, except for the cancer, and she could have lived well into old age. He said that her health was as good as any other woman her age and better than many.

After Mama died, Aunt Madge wanted to take Charlie, Susie and me to live with her in Seattle, Washington, but Papa wouldn't let her, and I am so glad he didn't. That would have been devastating to us. Although we loved Aunt Madge, we had only seen her a few times, and the thought of living in a city scared us to death. Besides that, to take us away from Papa and our brothers and sisters would have been a cruel thing to do.

Life with Papa

I never felt close to Papa like I did with Mama. I don't remember ever being hugged by him or him saying any words of affection. I don't remember seeing him hug any of us, but I was told that he did love the babies, and I had seen him play with his grandchildren and hug and kiss them.

Papa was strict about some things, especially boys. When I was fourteen, he embarrassed me to death by telling the neighborhood boys that if they ever fooled around with me he would take his shotgun to them. They believed him, and so did I.

Papa didn't want his daughters to wear makeup, not even lipstick. He said it made our lips look like "a possum's butt at pokeberry time."

Mama never wore any make up at all, and one time when Aunt Madge sent her some for Christmas, Papa got mad about it. Mama gave the makeup to Darlene, who used it, despite what Papa said. Darlene would give me her old lipsticks, and I loved that, but Mama didn't, as I would smear it all over my face, and even get it on my clothes.

I didn't attempt to wear makeup around Papa. In fact, I didn't wear much makeup when I was younger, and I still have a hard time putting on lipstick without thinking of that "possum's butt."

Papa told me he wanted me to concentrate on my education and not to run off and get married to some jackass. He said all my sisters had done that and look how they ended up. He said they all married guys that didn't have the brains of a piss-ant.

I refused dates my first two years of high school, but when I was a sophomore, there was one boy who came to the house even though I asked him not to.

PALERMO OFFICERS—Elected recently in a hotly contested political campaign are the new student body officers for Palermo Union School. They are front row, left to right, Ada Barker, secretary; Gloria Palmer and Barbara Cunningham, yell leaders. In back row, left, are Terry Carlson, president, and Richard Flatt, treasurer. (Mercury photo and …)

He came one day after school. Papa answered the door, and I was waiting for him to tell the boy to go away, but to my surprise, he didn't. He said I could go out and talk to the boy. I went out on the porch and talked to him for a while, and after he left, I went into the kitchen. I was sitting, eating an apple, when Papa came in and said that he thought the boy was very nice, and that maybe I could go to a movie with him some time.

I choked on the apple then, but Papa ignored my croaking and left the room. It took me awhile to digest what I heard—and the apple—

and I concluded that Papa was impressed because the boy was a senior and the president of his class.

I thought he was a nice boy, but I was somewhat afraid of him because he told me that every evening he would drive past my house several times and was tempted to stop—which he eventually did.

He had even said, "Since you won't go out with me, I guess I'll just have to kidnap you and take you off somewhere."

That scared the heck out of me, and I told Papa that. He said that he was sure that the boy was just kidding.

Papa was lonely after Mama died and spent hours in his room, listening to his radio and drinking wine.

Not too long after Mama's death, we had been to town and were on our way back home when Papa began talking about Mama. He said he wished he had treated her better, and the tears were running down his face. I had never seen him cry before.

Papa didn't take up with any woman after Mama died. I do remember, though, that he wrote to one of those lonely-hearts clubs and one of those women came to visit us.

She was kind of a big, tall woman and was nice enough, but none of us kids wanted her there. I especially didn't because she insisted on combing my hair, which was long, thick and always full of snarls. And, to top it all off, she told me that I should wear braids all the time. For heaven's sake, I was almost twelve and way too old for braids, which I never liked anyway.

After she left, we told Papa that we didn't want her to come back. He said not to worry, that she wore too much makeup and was bigger and stronger than he was. He never had another woman come around after that.

Joyride Gone Bad

In 1951, we lived in Hopland, California, in a big house on the top of a hill. It was a unique house; it had a dumb waiter that went from the dining room down to the kitchen, which was the only room below the rest of the house. It also had a player piano that sat on the wraparound porch. It was the grandest house we had ever lived in.

On one hot July afternoon, Jackie was sitting at the kitchen table having a cup of coffee, when Skippy and Jimmie came in from outside.

"What've you guys been doing out there?" Jackie asked.

"We fixed the flat tire on the convertible that Don Schragl left here," Skippy said as he went to the sink to wash up.

"We're going to hot wire it to get it started, and then we're going to go out to find work," Jimmie said.

Jackie had reservations. "It's too late in the day to do that. Besides, we don't have any money for gas."

Skippy said, "Maybe we can pawn that tire that's in the barn. It belongs to Papa's truck, so we'll have to leave before he gets home."

Jackie had a feeling that it wasn't going to be a job search, but he was willing to go along. He pushed his chair away from the table. "Okay, let's hit the road."

"I've gotta have something to eat," Skippy said. He picked up a jar of home-canned tomatoes that former occupants had left in the house.

Jackie said, "We should leave now. Papa might come home any minute."

"I'm starvin'. I've gotta eat something. I'm gonna make a bean sandwich."

"Make me one too," Jimmie said, "but don't put any of that crap on it. Darlene said we could get botulous from it."

"Botu-what?" Skippy asked.

"She said it could have botulism poison in it," Jackie said.

"Oh yeah, I remember that. We need to throw all that stuff out."

It was late afternoon when they got to the town of Hopland. They were lucky that the owner of the gas station let them have a tank of gas in exchange for the tire. He did that because he knew their father. After they gassed up the car, they took off toward Ukiah.

They stopped in Ukiah and had a cup of coffee at a café, then headed up a mountain road that led to a town called Covelo. Darkness had fallen, but the full moon made it almost as light as day.

A car came up behind them with its headlights on bright; it almost ran off the road as it whizzed past. There looked to be about four or five people inside.

"What the hell are they doing?" Skippy asked from the backseat.

"I don't know, but there's a little kid in there," Jackie said.

The car didn't get very far before it swerved off the road.

"Jesus, I think they went over," Jackie said.

When they got to where the car went off the road, they got out of the car and looked down the side of the mountain. To their surprise, they saw four men and a boy climbing up the mountain. Two of the men carried a case of beer between them.

When the men got up to the road, Jimmie said, "Man. we thought you'd all be killed."

"If anybody's hurt, we can take you to the hospital;" Jackie said.

146

One of the men said, "Nah, we're all okay."

"We can give you a lift," Jimmie said.

"Thanks, but family members will be coming along soon; we'll just wait here for them," one of the men carrying the beer said.

"Are you sure?" Jimmie asked.

"Yeah, we'll be okay. Hey, let us give ya each a beer. That's the least we can do for you guys for stopping to see about us."

Jackie surmised that alcohol was probably the reason for their accident, but he thought better of telling those big Indians that.

The boys took the beer and continued on their journey. It was a hot night, and as they clipped along, they were glad that they were in a convertible with the top down.

Around midnight, they were on a mountain road going to the tiny town of Elk Creek. Jackie had dosed off, and when he woke up, he was being thrown from the car as it flipped over and rolled down the mountain. He got knocked out when he landed on the mountainside. When he came to, he looked around for Jimmie and Skippy. Not seeing them, he hurried down to where the car had ended up. He found Jimmie lying near the creek at the bottom of the canyon.

Jimmie was dazed. "What happened?"

"I don't know. When I came to I was laying on the side of the mountain," Jackie said.

"Where's Skippy?"

"I don't see him. I'm gonna look for him as soon as I get you in the creek. The cool water will make you feel better."

Jackie got Jimmie to the creek, and then looked around for Skippy. He spotted Skippy's foot sticking out of the brush and heard him groaning.

He pulled back the brush and knelt beside him. "Damn, Skippy, are you in a lot of pain?"

"I hurt all over."

"I'm gonna get you down to the creek. Jimmie's already down there."

Jackie got Skippy to the creek, laid him beside Jimmie and said, "We've gotta get help. I'm gonna walk up the creek."

After walking about a mile, he saw an old cabin on the bank of the creek. It looked spooky, but he had to see if someone was there. He went up to the door and knocked. There was no answer but he continued to knock. A bullet whizzed past his head. He stood frozen for a few seconds, and then took off running back to where Jimmie and Skippy were. When he got to them, he dropped to the ground, gasping for air.

"Did you find someone to help us?" Jimmie asked.

Jackie told him what had happened.

"What're we gonna do? Skippy hasn't stopped moaning. I think he's hurt real bad," Jimmie said.

"I don't know," Jackie said, still catching his breath.

"We're gonna have to go back to that house; there might not be another house for miles. We gotta go with you. I heard a coyote howling a while ago, and it sounded awful close," said Jimmie

"I don't think Skippy can make it, " Jackie said.

"Then we've gotta carry him. We can't leave him here."

Skippy could barely walk, so Jackie and Jimmie carried him most of the way, stopping often to rest. Jimmie did this with a broken collarbone (which he didn't know at that time). The boys were uneasy as they approached the cabin. To their relief, an old man answered the door and invited them in.

"What're you boys doing here this time of night?" the wizened man asked, "and what's wrong with that young feller you're carrying?"

"He's hurt real bad. We had an accident and need to get help," Jackie said.

"Put him there on that cot. You other fellers sit there with him, whilst I fix ya somethin' to eat," the man said.

The sparsely furnished cabin had a cot, wood heater and a small table. A bucket of water sat on the table with a wash pan beside it. A rifle leaned against the wall, and Jackie was sure that it had to be the one that had sent a bullet past his head. He shuddered when he thought about what could have happened.

The man offered to lend them his old car but the car wouldn't start, so Jackie and Jimmie hiked up to the road to catch a ride to Nice, where their sister Darlene lived. They waited on the road a half hour before a car came along and gave them a ride.

Darlene contacted the sheriff in Hopland and asked if they could get a message to Papa, telling him what happened. Darlene and her husband, Bill, proceeded to take Jimmie and Jackie home, first stopping by their sister Edith's house to see if she could go to where Skippy waited. Edith and her husband picked up Skippy and took him to the hospital in Willows, where they found that he had a fractured pelvis bone.

The next morning, Papa took Jimmie to Dr. Craig in Lake County, who tried to put pins in Jimmie's broken collarbone with rusty pliers. After Papa told him in no way was he going to use those pliers, the

Doctor found a clean pair. The pins remained in Jimmie's collarbone for two years, and then were removed by the Marine Corps.

A strange thing happened August 16, 1955. We were at Edith's house, and Papa's nose started to bleed. When I saw the blood, a terrible chill came over me and I knew something terrible was going to happen. I got that feeling of dread that I always get in my prophetic dreams, and I wasn't the only one that felt that way — **Susie** did too. We never said anything to each other at the time, but we sensed what the other was feeling.

When it was time to go home, Papa took Charlie and Buddy, leaving Susie and me at Edith's, saying he would be back early the next morning and would bring stuff for breakfast.

The next morning we waited for him, and when he wasn't there by eleven o'clock, I knew something had happened to him.

Around noon, Buddy walked into the

house alone. He said that Papa had just been killed in an auto accident, and that **Charlie** was in the hospital, but wasn't seriously hurt. He said that the man that brought him home told him that Papa was dead.

Charlie received a cut under his arm that required quite a few stitches, but it wasn't too bad, and they released him from the hospital the next day. Papa was killed August 17, 1955. He was sixty-three years old.

After Papa's death, Charlie, Susie and I went to stay with Edith. We stayed with Edith for only a few months, and then she moved into a smaller house, so we went to live with our brother Cam and his wife, Mary, in Oakland. I loved being with Cam and Mary and their adorable little girls. They were so much fun.

Susie and Charlie had a tougher time. They were not used to big city schools, and they ended up going to live with other relatives. It was hard on them; they were both so young when Mama died, and to lose

Papa seven years later was difficult to overcome.

I was lonely when they left Oakland, and I was worried about them. It was a terribly sad time, and having them gone away from me, set me back to mourning not only Papa and Mama, but Bobby and Bud, as well. It was a long time before I could feel very happy about anything.

Ephriam and Mary Barker

EPILOGUE

Music & Poetry in the Blood

Many family members were good at singing and playing instruments, and I think there were a lot of missed opportunities in that field.

Bobby was a talented musician; he could play the guitar, harmonica and piano without ever having a lesson, and he didn't know a note of music. Johnny could sing just like Earnest Tubb, Paul had a great voice, and it was loud. I could hear him singing "Fireball Mail" from a mile away. He played the guitar as well. Skippy played the guitar and sang really well; he also wrote songs. Charlie sounded just like Elvis Presley, and he even looked like him. He had black hair and beautiful blue eyes and could smile just like Elvis. He was better than any of the Elvis imitators that I had ever seen.

I think they got their talent from Papa, he could play the five-string banjo like a pro, and he never had a lesson in his life. He learned to play from his father, who had learned to play from his father. I was so glad when my son Clint learned to play the banjo; it is kind of a family tradition.

The songs I remember the boys singing at the homestead were: Roy Acuff's "Fireball Mail," "Great Speckled Bird" and I believe, one entitled "Draw up the Papers Lawyer."

A couple of songs were gruesome, they were: "Don't Make Me Go to Bed & I'll be Good" and "Stone Cold Dead in the Market Place." A very sad one was "Old Shep," which would always bring a tear because that was our dog's name.

Throughout my life, music was very important to me. Mama said I started singing when I was around two, and was always singing. When I had access to a radio, I learned every word of the songs that were played. I especially liked Bing Crosby; his "Lily Marlene" and "Galway Bay" were my favorites. Two others that I liked were "Temptation" and "Far-away Places." It was so much fun singing "Temptation" that I was willing to sing it anytime, and one night Darlene woke me up to sing it for Johnny, who had come after

I was in bed and had to leave very early the next morning.

Back in our lineage was a young woman, **Elizabeth Barker,** whom Thomas Jefferson proposed marriage to; but she didn't accept and later married Colonel Ralston of North Carolina.

Also from our lineage is **Squire Omar Barker,** who has written hundreds of stories and poems and won two prized Spur awards from the Western Writers of America. He is best known for his poem, "A Cowboy's Christmas Prayer," about a cowhand's talk with God, from his 1954 book, "Songs of the Saddle." It is one of the most used verses for Christmas cards.

Omar was a forest ranger, as was his brother **Elliott.** In 1950, during a terrible forest fire in New Mexico, Elliott's crew found a bear cub clinging to a smoldering pine tree, with his fur singed and his footpads badly blistered. They made arrangements for the cub to be nursed back to health, and then Elliott turned *Smokey* over to the government with a provision that the bear's life be dedicated to wildlife conservation and fire prevention.

On Elliott's one-hundredth birthday, he made this statement: "I don't have an enemy in the world—I've outlived all those bastards."

We have some poets in our family, and I think Benny is the most prolific. Following are three of his, and four of mine. But the first one is by Great-grandmother Carrie E. Peterman, whose poems appeared occasionally in the periodical press, in Brush Creek, Iowa.

Carrie & Emery Peterman

The Road to Barkersville

AN AUTUMN PICTURE

We wandered one beautiful autumn day,
Away from the noisy town-
From the constant din of the busy streets
And the hurrying up and down.

When the sun was sinking low into the west
Like a dazzling ball of fire,
Peeping above the dark treetops
And lighting the tall church spire.

The breeze was soft as a lover's sigh,
Borne on the zephyr's wings,
And it whispered low, as it passed us by,
Pretty stories of woodland things.

It had sported about among the leaves
On many a summer day;
It had watched their growth from the tender bud
To the season of decay.
So we wandered on through grassy lanes
And beyond the busy mill,
To where the autumn leaves shone bright
And the river flowed calm and still.

And a heavenly peace was in our eyes
As we gazed on that woodland scene:
The trees with their gorgeous coloring
And the sparkling river between.

We watched the sun till it sank to rest,
Leaving naught but a fiery glow;
And the beautiful red of the sky o'erhead
Shone in the water below.

And the crickets chirped among the leaves,
And the shadows were falling down-
Shutting the scene from mortal eyes,
Ere we wandered back to town.

B. H. Barker

A TINY HAND IN MINE

Sometimes when he's unsteady in his step
Or there are stairs to climb,
He'll reach out to me and then he'll place
His tiny hand in mine.

And as I grip this tiny hand,
The feel of pleasure grows.
A feeling that I can't explain,
And some will never know.

I know that time will quickly pass,
And as the days move right along,
He'll grow into a fine young man
With a grip that's firm and strong.

But this memory will stay with me,
Not dimmed by age or time,
Etched in my mind forever,
His tiny hand in mine.

The Road to Barkersville

ROSES IN A BUCKET

With scissors and a bucket
She hurried from the room,
And went out to the roses
And began to cut the blooms.

She cut them oh so carefully
To save them any harm,
And then she placed them gently
In the bucket on her arm.

Then I felt kind of saddened
And I knew the reason why,
For the pretty, pretty roses
Would soon begin to die.

I know their days are numbered
Just as yours and mine,
But they would have lived much longer
If left upon the vine.

I suppose they'll bring some happiness,
And brighten up some rooms,
And eyes will shine with pleasure
When they see those pretty blooms.

So there is some consolation
That they'll make somebody glad,
But roses in a bucket
To me are kind of sad.

LET'S PRETEND

He'll come running up to me,
Then I'll hear him say,
"Come on, Grandpa,
"Let's go out and play."

And then I'll say, "What will we play?"
As if I didn't know

The Road to Barkersville

Because we'll play the same game
That we both love so.

We'll play the game of let's pretend
And fight the evil ones.
We'll chase away the Goose Bumps
And keep them on the run.

We have fought a thousand battles
From Mercury to Mars,
We have been on every planet
In the land above the stars.

We have been X-men and Power Rangers,
And other heroes too:
Like Batman, Robin, Superman
Just to name a few.

We had such wondrous times
As our little games we played,
And to see the look upon his face,
These memories will never fade.

Because I know the time will come
When this game will surely end,
And there will be no little one to say,
"Grandpa, let's pretend."

The Road to Barkersville

ME

I have laughed with the best,
And cried with the worst;
Most times feeling lucky,
Sometimes feeling cursed.

I have loved much too strongly,
And hated the same;
You can trust what I tell you,
I won't play a game.

I take full blame for what I've become,
Equal to most, inferior to some.
I've had lots of joy, and equal of pain,
But all in all, I can't complain.

RICH LITTLE POOR GIRL

I may look a little bedraggled,
Like a homeless waif no doubt;
But when I pretend that I'm a lady,
I am finessed as all get out.

A prince in shining armor,
Trots up to me and sees,
That I am the finest lady,
And falls upon his knees.

He begs me for my hand, he does,
And offers me the world,
But it is already mine, you see,
So these words to him I hurled.

My gold is in the morning sun,
My silver is the moon.
My diamonds are the drops of dew
Upon the rose's bloom.

I hold reign over the hillside,
And all the flowers so blue,

And I would love to run barefoot
Through those flowers with you.

I have it all right here; I do,
I couldn't leave without a care,
For the joys I've known are many
And can't be found just anywhere.

LET THE CHILDREN LAUGH AND PLAY

When my life on earth does cease,
And I have my hard earned peace;
Just lay me in a box of pine,
And gather those I left behind.
All kith and kin that really cared,
With whom the joys of life I shared;
Let those who wish, have their say,
And let the children laugh and play.

Don't have someone I do not know,
Saying things that just aren't so;
Let those I loved, who loved me,
When speaking of what used to be;
Dwell only on the good times had,
And put aside all that was bad.
But the most important thing this day:
Let the children laugh and play.

As you go and leave me now,
To yourselves please make this vow:
To always do all that you can
For every precious child of man.
Cast out those who children hate,
Let misery be their only fate.
And most of all make safe the way,
To let the children laugh and play.

After I'm laid in the ground,
If you should ever come around
To lay some flowers at my head,
Remember all the words I've said.

The Road to Barkersville

Let the little ones come close,
Keep spirits high; don't be morose,
And should they scamper where I lay,
Let the children laugh and play.

TWENTY-ONE TODAY

As I left for work
That summer afternoon,
My head was filled with happy thoughts
Of what would happen soon.
For not only was I turning twenty-one today,
Tonight I would be proposing
To my girlfriend, Liza Rae.

Into my pocket, I put the ring
I had bought the day before,
Kissed my mother on the cheek,
And headed out the door.
At Tony's Pizza where I worked
To pay my way through school,
I went around all afternoon
Grinning like a fool.

Friends came in and chided me,
Said I would ruin my life.
They said that all my fun would end
The day I took a wife.
But I only knew I was on my way
To fulfilling all my dreams,
A wife, a home, kids and career,
Were all possible now it seemed.

The clock on the wall read 9:45,
Almost time to close,
And with every passing moment,
The excitement grows and grows.
I was just starting toward the back
When I heard someone come in,
I turned to face a snubbed nose gun,
Held by a man so tall and thin.

The Road to Barkersville

I looked into his empty eyes,
And froze just where I stood.
The nervous man, voice trembling said:
"No one gets hurt if this goes good."
Next thing I knew there was a blast,
And I crumpled to the floor.
A terrible pain seared through my chest,
Then there was one blast more.

I felt something fall beside me,
And I looked over to see,
The empty eyes now filled with fear
Were looking back at me.
He reached over and laid his hand
Upon my bloody chest.
"God, this can't be happening;
I made it through the rest."

His voice was but a whisper,
But I could hear what he had to say:
"You know, it's my birthday,
I'm twenty-one today."
I grabbed his hand; he gave a jerk,
His eyes rolled in his head,
And everything was going black,
I knew we were both dead.

THE FACES IN MY HEAD

I close my eyes and faces appear.
    Kind, sad, strong—none smiling.
Who are they? I don't recognize them.
    Have I seen them in passing or pictures?
They captivate me; I don't know why.
    Are they the hermit souls from Walter Foss's
"House by the Side of the Road?"
    Or the rolling stones from Robert Service's
"The Men That Don't Fit in?"
    Oh, wouldn't that be the grandest gift:
To see poetry as well as hear?

THE SHADOWS OF LIFE

There are those who wait in the shadows of life;
For what do they wait in their world full of strife?
For the love and comfort of those who should care;
Those who see but pretend they're not there.
But they are there all around us wherever we go,
With eyes full of sorrow and heads that hang low.
So if you should see them, pause for a while,
To offer a kind word or perhaps just a smile.
Life plays no favorites and someday you may wait,
In the shadows of life by some act of fate.

ADA AND I

Ada and I live in the same body.
Ada and I share the same soul.
But Ada and I differ quite often
About what is each one's roll.

Ada thinks she is the strong one,
I thinks that Ada's too weak.
Ada thinks I is too arrogant,
Trying to mask that she's meek.

Myself thinks they are both wrong
And should try to be more like Me,
Who always tries to compromise
Even though they ignore her plea.

APPENDIX

Generations

My ancestors arrived in America in the 1600s and settled in Virginia. The Washington county Surveyors Record's places my lineage in Washington County in the 1700s, and that is where the following ancestors were born.

1

Edward Barker: born about 1698 in London England; died in Virginia soon after coming to the Colonies. Married **unknown**.

11

John Barker: born about 1732 in St. Paul's Parish, Hanover County, Virginia; died after 1782. Married **Martha Snead** in 1759 in Hanover County, Virginia. Martha was born in 1735 in Surry County, Virginia; died in 1796 in Washington County, Virginia at age 61.

111

Rev. Thomas O. Barker: born 1760 in Hanover County, Virginia; died before March 14, 1845. He married **Rebecca Gaddy**, daughter of **Sherwood Gaddy** and **Mary Bright**, in 1776 in Bedford County, Virginia. Rebecca was born in 1754 in Bedford County, Virginia, and died on Feb 3, 1841, in Virginia at age 87.

Treasury warrants were given for tracks of land to men who fought in the American Revolution by the King of Great Britain's Proclamation of 1863, and the Virginia Land Warrant of May 1777.

Great-great-great-great grandfather **Thomas O. Barker** was a recipient of land under these warrants. He was a soldier in the Revolutionary War under General George Washington, and fought at Landy's Lane. He served for seven years. The first documented was a survey for 30 acres in Washington County on December 21, 1781. The second was a survey for 100 acres made on April 22,1782.

Also receiving land by these warrants were Thomas's brother's, **John** and **Charles,** who fought with the Over Mountain Men in the Revolutionary War of Kings Mountain.

1V

Charles "Zet" Barker: born about 1779 in Russell County, Virginia; died before Sept. 10, 1849, in Washington County, Virginia. Married

Katherine Chiles; born about 1782 in Pennsylvania County, Virginia; died in 1852 in Mendota, Washington County, Virginia.

V

Thomas D. Barker: born April 26, 1806, in Washington Co, Virginia; died July 16, 1889, in Kinderhook Dist. Washington County, Virginia. Cause of Death: Fell from a roof, and injured with a knife He married **Permelia Newton** in 1823 in Washington County, Virginia. Permelia was born on Sep 19, 1806, in Kentucky and died on Nov 17, 1873, in Washington County, Virginia at age 67. Inscription on her grave reads "Thy Will Be Done"

V1

Henry Barker: born 1834 in Washington County, Virginia; died June 09, 1908, in Washington County, Virginia, from an accidental self-inflicted gunshot wound. Married (1) **Ellen Baker** (I/2 Blackfoot Indian): born 1837 in Virginia; died April 6, 1866, in Washington County, Virginia. Henry married (2) **Elizabeth Mead** (or **Maddox or Minnick**) before 1870. He married (3) **Elizabeth Jane Wyatt** March 02, 1871.

Henry joined the confederate Army in the Civil war along with his brother-in-law, **James Pinkston**, and **Will Chiles**. They deserted. Two of Henry's brothers, **Granville** and **Thomas**, were shot and killed for not enlisting with the South.

V11

Rev. Campbell Heiskel Barker Sr. was born on Aug 10, 1858, in Kinderhook, Washington County, Virginia, and died on Jan 8, 1931, in Sacramento, California, at age 72.

Campbell married **Fairzina "Gal" Good Hensley**, daughter of **Lilburn Hensley** and **Lucinda Good Hensley**, on Sep 27, 1877, in Abingdon, Washington County, Virginia. Fairzina was born on Jul 19, 1861, in Scott County, Virginia, and died on Jun 11, 1953, in Graton, Sonoma County, California at age 91.

General Notes: Oroville Mercury, January 12, 1931: *Former Baptist Minister dead. Funeral service will be held here Wednesday at 1:30 pm for the late Rev. Campbell H. Barker former resident of the Pentz district. (Butte Co.). Barker who has been living in Sacramento for the last ten years died in the Capital City Monday. The body will arrive Wednesday and burial will be in Thermalito IOOF Cemetery under direction of Hamilton Riley.*

Survivors are wife and nine children. Reverend Barker was a member of Hilton, Virginia Lodge #312 Odd Follows and a retired Baptist minister. He was aged 74 years.

General Notes: *Woman Who Left 171 Descendants Is Buried in*

Thermalito, Butte County. Mrs. Fairzina Barker, 93, who died in Sebastopol, Sonoma County, June 1, 1953, was the forbear of 171 descendants surviving to the fourth generation. Funeral services were conducted here today, June 14, 1953, for the widow of Rev. C. H. Barker of Oroville and interment was in the Odd Fellows Cemetery in Thermalito. The Hamilton-Riley Mortuary had charge. Mrs. Barker was the Mother of Ben H., Seaton, and Ephriam Barker, both of Oroville, C. H. Jr. of Chico and Mrs. Lily Tregoning of Graton, Sonoma County. 64 grandchildren, 95 great grandchildren and 8 great-great grandchildren also survive her.

The Children of Campbell and Fairzina:

V111

Cordelia: born Apr 28, 1879, in Washington County, Virginia; died on Apr 20, 1905, in Washington County, Virginia at age 25. Cordelia married **William Wolford Barger** on Dec 24, 1895, in Washington County, Virginia.

Henry Clay: born Dec 12, 1881, in Washington County, Virginia; died on Aug 30, 1944, in Washington County, Virginia at age 62. Henry married **Nina "Bettie" Barker**, daughter of **Solomon Lewis Barker** and **Harriet E Dove**, on Feb 13, 1899, in Washington County, Virginia. Nina was born on Aug 14, 1879, in Washington County, Virginia, and died on Jan 23, 1947, in Washington County, Virginia at age 67.

Bertha Virginia: born Dec 18, 1883, in Washington County, Virginia; died on Oct 7, 1941, in Washington County, Virginia at age 57. Bertha married **Mark Dorton Shankle** in 1899. Bertha next married **Carl Sidney Bailey** in 1900. Bertha next married **George F Brown**.

Campbell Heiskel Jr.: born Sep 19, 1886, in Mendota, Washington, Virginia; died on Oct 6, 1963, in Paradise, Butte County, California at age 77. Campbell married **Ada Florence Palmer** on Jul 13, 1912, in Warm Beach, Snohomish County, Washington.

Benjamin Harrison: born Aug 9, 1888, in Abrams Falls, Washington County, Virginia; died on Apr 10, 1979, at age 90. He never married.

Seaton Graves: born Jan 12, 1894, in Abrams Falls, Washington County, Virginia; died on Nov 15, 1968, in Fort Bragg, Mendocino County, California at age 74. Seaton married **Mary Viola Palmer** on Mar 14, 1913, in Everett, Snohomish County, Washington. Seaton next married **Minnie Olivia Robinson** on Jan 21, 1924, in Sacramento, Sacramento County, California.

Lillie May: born on May 10, 1896, in Abrams Falls, Washington County, Virginia; died on Aug 16, 1979, in Santa Rosa, Sonoma County, California at age 83. Lillie married **Richard Noel Reed** on Sep 14,

1913, in Simmons Hop Ranch, Mission Bottoms, Marion Co., Oregon. Lillie next married **Orville Tregoning** on Apr 3, 1944.

Earl Clifton: born on Aug 9, 1899, in Washington County, Virginia; died from tuberculosis on Mar 31, 1921, in Butte County, California at age 21.

Ephriam Buck: born May 1, 1892, in Abrams Falls, Washington County, Virginia; died on Aug 17, 1955, in Sebastopol, Sonoma County, California at age 63. Ephriam married **Mary Henrietta Peterman**, daughter of **Chauncey Lewis Peterman** and **Margaret McWilliams**, on Sep 14, 1913, in Simmons Hop Ranch, Mission Bottoms, Marion County, Oregon. Mary was born on May 22, 1898, in South Dakota, and died on Aug 18, 1948, in Colusa Memorial Hospital, Colusa, California at age 50.

Ephriam Barker and Mary Peterman had twenty children:

IX

August Leonard: born August 20, 1914; died from typhoid January 12, 1922, at age seven.

Elden Ephriam (Bud): born October 31, 1916; died from auto accident May 25, 1953, at age 36. He married **Leora Murphy**, and they had no children. He became involved with his brother Bobby's wife, **Mary Gash**, a few months after Bobby's death and had two children with her—**Eldena** and **Ann**. Bud was killed near Arbuckle. He was riding with four other men, including his brother Pat; they had all been drinking all day. One other man was also killed.

Ruth Mary: born June 6, 1918; died from typhoid on January 4, 1922, at age three.

Earl Clifton: born Sept. 30, 1919. Married **Doris Koenig** on April 27, 1940, and they had two children—**Carol** and **Gary**.

Edith Viola: born Dec. 10, 1920; died April 3, 1975, from cervical cancer at age 55. She married **William Francis**, and they had five children—**Shirley, Mary, William, Barbara,** and **Lonna**. Edith had a brief fling with her cousin, **Jess Reed**, and they had a child—**Jessie Noel**, who died as an infant. Her second marriage was to **Don Schragl**, and they had one child—**Donna**.

John David: born April 10, 1922; died May 1, 2002. He was eighty years old and had a few health problems, such as a bad heart, prostate cancer, and melanoma. However, his mind was still very alert, and he was telling his stories right up to the end. Johnny married **Eileen Rose**, and they had five children—**John, Sherry, Pamela, Lynette,** and **Rebecca**.

Robert Granville: born August 25, 1923; died from accidental gunshot on Feb. 19, 1950. He married **Mary Gash** in 1947, and they had two children—**Kathleen** and **Mary Susan**. Bobby was killed pulling a double barrel shotgun out of his car. It went off, striking him in the chest. He had his wife and two baby girls with him; he was 26 years old.

Theodore: born January 13, 1925. He married **Alice Grant** Oct. 20, 1942. They had twelve children—**Theodore, Patsy, Joy, Joe,** twins: **Steve** and **Arlene,** and **Warren, Ross, Ronald, Peggy, Lyle** and **Carl.**

Patrick Henry: born March 24, 1926; died November 13, 1978, in Oroville, California due to pulmonary emphysema with neumenitis. He was 52 years old. He married **Bonny Gash** in 1949, and they had five children—**Michael, Debra, Elden, Glenda** and **Cindy.**

Campbell Heiskel 3: born Nov. 5, 1927; died Sept. 5, 1983, in a boating accident at Clear Lake, California at age 56. He married **Mary Ruth Madden** on Sept. 17, 1950. They had two children—**Cammy** and **Karen.** His second marriage was to **Linda Allan**; they had no children.

Benjamin Harrison 2: born Nov. 14, 1928. He married **Mildred Rose** on Sept 8, 1950. They had two children—**Janice** and **Richard.**

Darlene Virginia: born August 31, 1930; died on September 23, 1992, of complications from alcohol. She married **Adrian "Bill" Thomson** in 1948, and they had three children—**Adrian "Nick", Shawn** and **Daniel "Brian".**

Paul: born Dec. 17, 1931. He married **Phyllis Bond** on November 18, 1954, and they had four children—**Forrest, Jeffery, Lisa** and **Rafe.**

Gloria: born Jan 25, 1933; died from lung cancer in Dec. of 2000 at age 67. She married **Mathew Wallen** and they had three children—**Theresa, Jennifer** and **David.** Her second marriage was to **Joe Ballez** and they had seven children—**Brenda, Andrea, Tina, Tony, Christopher, Shelly** and **Guy.** Her third marriage was to **Reed Howery** and they had one son—**Cory.**

Five of Gloria's children came to a tragic end: David drowned while trying to rescue a cousin. Jenny was killed in an auto accident, being crushed underneath a car. Tony was stabbed to death trying to protect his cousin Cara from a crazed man. Guy was murdered at Cara's house, over something to do with drugs, and Chris was killed in an auto accident that severely injured his son.

Jackie: born June 26, 1934. He married **Shirley Hinds** on Nov. 22, 1952, and they had three children—**Jack, Casey** and **Loretta.** His second marriage was to **Marjorie Sailor** and they raised Jackie's grandson, **Chief,** Marjorie's children and several foster children.

Jimmie: born June 26, 1934. He married **Myrna Houghton** June 6, 1953, and they had four children—**Jim, Timothy, Shane** and **Samuel.**

Franklin Delano (Skippy): born Dec. 9, 1935; died June 15, 1979, when his jeep rolled over a cliff in Bidwell Park in Chico, CA. He was 44 years old. He married **Edith Wallen** and they had three children— **Mark, Julie** and **Ephriam**.

Ada Florence: born April 28, 1938. She married **James William Underhill** on May 18, 1958. They had six children—**Clinton James, Gregory William, Jill Maureen, Todd Bentley, Lori Beth** and **Marléna Colleen**. They were divorced on May 18, 1978. She married **Manuel Guyot** on October 31, 1978, and they had no children.

Charles Louis: born December 30, 1940; died in April of 1990 from a stroke. He was 49 years old. He married **Betty Free**, and they had nine children—**Kelly, Lyle, Carl, Elden, Cara, Scott, Marvis and twins Vincent** and **Vaughn.**

Susan Jane: born April 12, 1942. She married **Del Howard** and they had three children—**Jane, Sandra and Diane**. Her second marriage was to **Ronald Smith** and they had three children—**Robin, Derick** and **Lance**.

ABOUT THE AUTHOR

ꟼda F. Barker

Ada Florence Barker was born and raised in California and spent the first eight years of her life at the family homestead in Barkersville, running those mountains from daylight till dark with her brothers and sisters. They didn't have much in the way of material things, but what they did have was priceless — they had what nature provided, their imaginations as playthings, and the freedom to use them.

Printed in the United States
150839LV00009B/162/P

9 780615 194516